The Story of My Life

"It's great to be me!"

Alicia de Haas

(with Peter de Haas)

For my family

© 2022 de Haas Publishing

ISBN: 978-0-646-85945-3

All rights reserved. No part of this publication may be reproduced, distributed or transmitted in any form or by any means, including photocopying, recording or imaging or by any other electronic or mechanical methods, without the prior written permission of the author and publisher, except in the case of brief quotations embodied in critical reviews and certain other non-commercial uses permitted by copyright law.

Copy editing and interior design by
All-read-E (http://philipnewey.com/All-read-E.htm)

Cover design by Glen Holman (glenholman.com),
To protect the privacy of extended family and friends named in this book, surnames have been omitted.

A catalogue record for this work is available from the National Library of Australia

Table of Contents

Introduction 1
Born to be Alive! 3
Childhood Years 16
Teenager … 38
Our "Tree Change" … and Other Great Adventures 45
My Thirtieth Birthday Holiday 58
Special Pastoral Assistant 65
A Slower Pace … but with Big Interests 68
Now: Life is Good, and it is Good to be Me! 73
Stories by Family and Friends 80
My Story … My Gift 90

Introduction

Hi, my name is Alicia Nicole de Haas, and I am very happy to welcome you into this little book about my life. I am very excited that my book will be available to my dear family and friends, all of whom I love very much. However, I want to tell *everyone* my story, from the time I was born till today when I am enjoying my life as a thirty-eight-year-old woman living with my adoptive parents, Peter and Angela, in Mareeba, in Far North Queensland.

I have Down's Syndrome, with some intellectual and physical disabilities (especially problems with my heart) which have been present since I was born … but this hasn't stopped me at all from living a very full and rich life, filled with much love, joy and laughter—and with lots of adventures. While I do have some disabilities, I have many more abilities. I am looking forward to telling you about some of these …

My dad, Peter, has already published two books so I thought to myself, why not another one … this time about little old me 😊? So I asked him, and after some careful thought over a few weeks—given that this will be a big project—he agreed. Thank you, Dad!

As far as possible, I would like to tell my story with my own words, but I realise that this will not always work out. Sometimes I might just be too tired, or not in the mood to think or help when Peter is writing my book. That's OK, I trust him … most of the time … and will check carefully whatever he writes, as will my mum … **very carefully.**

I have also received a warning from one of my aunties: "Alicia, you make sure you read all your father's writing. Don't let him be too silly!"

There are some parts of my story that I simply couldn't know because I was only a baby, or a young child, so I will need to rely on the memory of my parents, and other sources, to tell these parts. That's fine by me.

At the very start of this book, I want to say how much I appreciate the love and the wonderful care my parents, our extended families, and my friends, have given to me over the years. You are all an integral part of this story. Without you, there wouldn't be much of a story to tell. I especially want to acknowledge, thank and honour my mum, Angela, who has been my primary carer for all of my life, day in and day out, except for my first fourteen days when I was in hospital in Brisbane. She is my very best friend, just so special to me, way beyond anything I can put into words.

Also, I would like to acknowledge my birth parents, Diana and Neville (dec.) who gave me the greatest gift of all: life. Diana is Peter's youngest sister. When I was born, she and Neville felt that they didn't have the capacity to give me the high level of care that I would need over a long time. So they felt it would be best if I was put up for adoption. That's OK; I understand; it all worked out very well for me. I am having a good life and am happy with it … and I am happy to be **me**.

So, let's get on with my story.

(*Note by Peter, the editor*: It has been interesting writing this first page because Alicia keeps coming in and asking: *How's it going, Dad?* She is just about "jumping out of her skin" so it will be fascinating to see how she goes over the next few weeks [months, probably] as her life story is being written, edited and published. I may have to lock the door! Seriously, though, I really want Alicia to be happy with the telling of her story, so I will be seeking her approval, one page at a time, which is what she will be able to cope with.)

Born to be Alive!

I picked this title myself. I hope you like it.

What to do with me?

I was born on 20 May 1983, at 10.50 am, in the Royal Brisbane Women's Hospital, weighing 2950 grams and measuring 46.5 centimetres, a very small baby. Of course, it didn't take long for the hospital staff to realise that I had Down's Syndrome. This came as a huge shock to my birth parents, Diana and Neville, who had no indications at all before then that I would have this condition, and its associated disabilities. They were expecting another completely healthy baby to add to their little family of three, Damian being my older brother who turned two a week after I was born.

In a letter to Peter and Angela, dated 24 May 1983, Peter's mother, Corry de Haas (nee Siemons) informed them of my arrival and explained what happened next:

> … And now, I have to tell you some bad news. Diana gave birth to a little baby girl on Friday 20th, but the poor little mite is a Down's Syndrome baby. You will understand the agony and heartbreak this has caused to Diana and Neville. Dad and I are knocked senseless by this new blow and feel right out of our depth. You sometimes wonder if there is a god. They've worked so hard and had a beautiful room ready and were so happy to have another baby. And so many little ones are born each day to parents that don't even want them.
>
> After a lot of soul searching and discussions with welfare officers and social workers, Diana and Neville decided that they would make the

break now and give the baby up for adoption. What agony this caused them you could only understand if you are a mother yourself …

I saw the little baby on Sunday, and she looks very much like Damian, lovely blond hair. I dearly wished I could have held it for just a moment, but I feel more at peace now since I have seen it. Diana didn't want us to visit her in hospital, so we did as she wished …

After a day or two recovering from her labour, Diana went home feeling very sad, and I remained in the hospital. I was now completely dependent on the care and attention of the medical staff, while my future—my life—hung in the balance.

> … *my future—my life—hung in the balance …*

Angela and Peter received his mother's letter on Friday 27 May, a week after I was born, and this was the first time they knew of my existence, although they didn't know my name. It wasn't in the letter. They had been trying to have a baby for some years but, after several invasive tests, and feeling they weren't going anywhere, had decided "enough was enough". They had already been thinking about adoption, and Peter had also been praying to be blessed with their own child. When the letter arrived from Peter's mother, they were both in shock, but almost at once Peter started asking himself: *I have been praying for a child. Could this be the answer to my prayers? Is God saying, well, what about this little baby girl?*

Angela had spent several years working with children and young people with disabilities, so she already knew that, while a full-time caring role would be demanding, such people (like me 😊) often have something very, very special: the ability not only to give a great deal of love, with no strings attached, but also to draw love from others, even from some of the hardest cases. Peter hadn't had the same experience, and in an earlier conversation that year, when discussing the possibility of

> *I could never adopt a baby or a child with a disability.*
>
> *Peter*

adoption, had told Angela: *I could never adopt a baby or a child with a disability.* As they say, famous last words!

That night, they went to a bush dance with their very good (lifelong) friends Rob and Lynne (who would later become my godparents), but their hearts and minds weren't in the dancing at all. They were concerned about me, alone in the hospital in Brisbane and obviously facing a very uncertain future. So there was a lot of talking, especially with Rob and Lynne, and not much dancing.

After a very restless and mostly sleepless night, Angela and Peter decided that they wanted to explore the possibility of adoption. This was now occupying all of their thinking and emotions. After spending some further time considering the pros and cons with Rob and Lynne, they called my birth parents to see if they might consider a family adoption.

They were very surprised to receive this call as they hadn't expected anyone within the extended family to be interested in adopting me. While Neville was open to the idea, Diana was initially more hesitant, grappling with whether it would be better to have a complete break and not know what happened to me, or to have the adoption take place within the family so that she could know where I was—and how I was doing—with the possibility of some contact in future. They told Peter and Angela that they would think about it for a day or so.

Later that same day, Peter called his parents and two of his sisters, Brigitte and Veronique. They were both somewhat surprised by the offer to adopt me, but that quickly changed to being very supportive.

Peter's father, however, wasn't keen on the idea at all. Amongst other things, he was concerned about the impact on Peter's career as an Army Officer by the demands of caring for me. So the day finished with Peter's and Angela's stomachs churned up with all the emotions and issues of having to assimilate the reactions of Peter's parents, while also waiting to learn what Diana and Neville's decision would be.

After another restless night—with the minds and hearts of at least four people very active—Neville called early the following morning (Sunday) to say that he and Diana were prepared to consider Peter and Angela's offer to adopt me but felt that it was necessary to first have a decent "heart to heart" conversation to discuss the various aspects and issues involved. This was quickly agreed upon, and plans were then put in motion for Peter and Angela to drive to Brisbane early the following week. They were elated and excited after this phone call.

Then it quickly dawned upon them that they had absolutely nothing organised for me, a very cute and very tiny little baby: no clothes, no nappies, no room, no bed … nothing. This needed to be fixed. So, thinking about, or making, all the necessary arrangements consumed the rest of the day, and continued well into the night. Peter recorded that he and Angela were still up at midnight, and that by then they had drunk half a flagon of port!

The next day being Monday, a normal working day, Peter put on his Army major's uniform and went to work as usual at Joint Communications-Electronics Branch, HQ Australian Defence Force, but he was feeling absolutely shattered after the goings on over the weekend. He briefed his bosses on what was happening, and was immediately granted emergency leave, being told: *Take as long as you need*. Now isn't that nice?

Meanwhile, Angela was very busy running around to friends and shops getting the essentials together. Everyone was just so generous and supportive in making sure she and Peter had all the things they would need to care for me. That evening, most of these bought and donated items were packed into their car and, very early the next morning, Peter and Angela left their home in Canberra to drive to Brisbane … feeling excited and anxious at the same time.

On the following day, Wednesday, Diana, Neville, Peter and Angela spent many hours together discussing—in great depth—the options for my adoption and the implications of each one. Peter recorded that this involved some deep "soul searching" by each of them, as well as complete openness and honesty. He wrote about this day as being a very enriching experience.

During this lengthy conversation, Diana and Neville confirmed they would not be able to cope with caring for me. Peter and Angela noted their circumstances were very different, and they felt they could provide me with the care and love I needed. If they could not have children of their own—which seemed likely—being entrusted to love and care for me would be a great act of love by Diana and Neville. So, in the end, late that afternoon, Diana and Neville agreed that Peter and Angela could adopt me. Arrangements were then made to meet in the afternoon of the next day (Thursday) so that I could be taken from the nursery in the hospital, where I had been since my birth, and given to Peter and Angela.

My New Family ... those First Days

The following morning, they met with the paediatrician at the Royal Brisbane Women's hospital. She told Peter and Angela about my heart murmur, what they could expect about my development, and my likely life span (since proved very wrong). This unexpected news made them sad, as it would be another big challenge I (and they) would have to face, with very uncertain outcomes. Peter records that the doctor was quite emotional herself when she was speaking to them. Nevertheless, this news didn't affect their decision to go ahead with my adoption.

> *... late in the afternoon of Thursday 2 June 1983, fourteen days after I was born, Peter and Angela became my foster parents, and I was entrusted into their care.*

After having lunch with Diana and Neville, they all went back to the hospital to collect me from the nursery. Diana did this by herself and then brought me down to the foyer of the hospital where Neville was waiting with Peter and Angela. Diana then gave me to them, and so, even though there was nothing in writing and no formal adoption papers—that would happen months later—from that moment, late in the afternoon of Thursday 2 June 1983, fourteen days after I was born, Peter and Angela became my foster parents, and I was entrusted into their care. As you might imagine, this was a very poignant moment for all of them.

For the next three days, my new family stayed with Peter's sister Veronique (who I know as Aunty Kiki) and her husband Darryl in Brisbane. Fortunately, Kiki was a trained and experienced midwife and had already had a baby herself (my cousin Jade). Peter and Angela, who didn't have the opportunity to attend any pre-natal courses—and were, therefore, really quite clueless about how to care for me—learnt a great deal from Veronique. Slowly they grew in confidence, and even Peter could competently change my nappies by the third day.

What became clear very quickly was the difficulties I was having in feeding. I could only take quite tiny amounts of milk formula, and that very, very slowly. Quite often, after spending a long time feeding, I would bring most of it back up and would then be too tired to try again. Peter, who has always loved his food, was often very worried about me not having enough to eat, especially since he couldn't just "fix it" and therefore felt completely powerless most of the time. That wouldn't be the last time I freaked him out. Peter continued to worry a great deal about my feeding, as did Angela, for many months.

On 6–7 June, we drove home to Canberra with an overnight stop. I travelled very well, sleeping most of the way on both days. Then, late on Tuesday 7 June, together with my adoptive parents, I arrived at my first home address (there would be more all around Australia) in Flynn, ACT.

That First Night ... by Veronique (Aunty Kiki)

Watching my brother lift Alicia into his arms for the first time after arriving in our home, I saw him completely overwhelmed with emotion and nerves, but the look of love he gave Alicia still brings tears to my eyes now. With Angela looking over his shoulder, I felt like I was witnessing something from Bethlehem and The Holy Family, except Jesus was a tiny girl. I knew immediately that Alicia would always be in safe, if somewhat shaky, hands and they would do whatever it took to love and care for her and give her every opportunity to thrive.

It is difficult to explain what I was feeling the very first time we met our niece, Alicia. Her tiny rosebud mouth, with her even tinier little tongue, poking out between her lips, her eyelids graced with tiny white lashes at a slightly downward curve, her little ears hidden by the baby blanket she was wrapped in, lying in the bassinet. Alicia was tinier than our own daughter at birth.

The first night had challenges, as even though I had explained how to handle a newborn, both Peter and Angela were very nervous, as would be expected, and, as any baby knows, when the parents are nervous, you cry. I don't think any of us slept much that first night, or for several nights ...

Over the ensuing days, both new parents became more comfortable with changing and feeding, the routine of catching sleep when you could—if anyone knows my brother, he does not function well at all without sleep or food. Angela took to her new motherly role with a more relaxed outlook and was soon comfortable with doing all the regular changes, feeding, bathing. I don't want to dwell on the challenges, but they were significant, as Alicia also had serious heart issues. We had to be careful that she fed enough to get her nourishment, but not to the point of exhaustion—it was a very fine balance.

Some nights I would sit up with either Angela or Peter while they fed Alicia or, if she was crying, taking her for a walk around the house, so they could have a bit of rest.

Settling Down Together

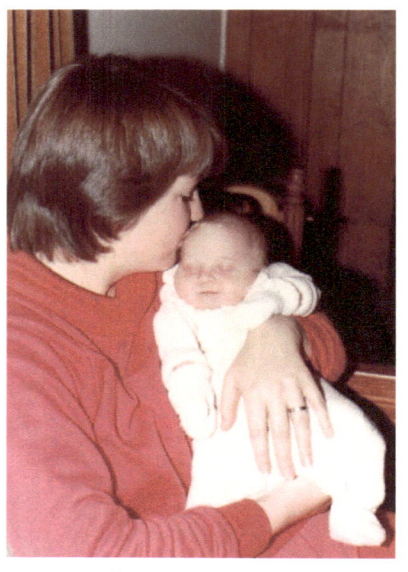

Safe in Angela's arms.

Now our new life together as a little family could begin …

I continued to have big problems with feeding, both in having the energy to suck on the bottle, and in keeping the milk formula down. It was a constant and frustrating struggle for all of us, which would continue for many months. Nevertheless, I was making some progress, growing a little and gradually putting on weight. From 2–9 June, I gained 35 g and grew a little, which made Angela and Peter very happy.

In those first weeks, initial appointments were made with paediatricians, social workers and physiotherapists, and further tests were booked for my heart murmur. So, the ongoing professional attention and care that I would need was very quickly put into place.

Presents from family and friends kept rolling in. As Peter and Angela let more of them know of my arrival, the support we were given as a family was truly remarkable and humbling for them. At the same time, the bond of love within our little family was steadily growing, and Peter and Angela were already very happy with me. Even now, I was responding to the stimulating rattles, mobiles and other toys in and around my cot.

Slowly, the days rolled into weeks and the weeks faded into months as I made steady progress, despite my ongoing struggles with feeding. I hadn't reached ten pounds after eight weeks!

As early as 19 June, my Aunty Mona (Peter's oldest sister) arrived from Brisbane to see me for the first time. She was very supportive of the decision Peter and Angela had made with Diana and Neville for my adoption … and she loved me from the moment she laid eyes on me.

I was baptised into the Catholic Church on 3 July 1983. Rob and Lynne were (and still are) my wonderful god parents. Of all Peter and Angela's friends, they were most encouraging and supportive in these first days and weeks, firstly in coming to the decision to explore the possibility of my adoption, and then in supplying what was needed in so many practical ways.

After my baptism, with my godparents.

Then, not too many days later, I gave Peter and Angela my first smile. By then I was also sleeping through the night, which made life a little easier for them. But not for long …

Highs and Lows

Heart failure!

Peter was away on an Army training course when it happened … I had a heart failure, a serious and alarming setback which created a huge amount of stress and panic for my foster parents, and also alarmed my paediatrician. As a result, I was placed on a regular dose of Digoxin (a heart stimulant) and, after a while, this helped to stimulate and stabilise my heart. This episode certainly reminded everyone, if they needed reminding, how fragile and tenuous my life was at this time.

On a more positive note, I was now really starting to respond to my environment, being very active while awake, and I was also starting to gurgle and talk. My paediatrician was very pleased with this and told Peter and Angela that my constant alertness, responsiveness and activity were all very promising signs.

Meanwhile, all tests on my heart were now completed. These revealed that I have what is known as an A-V canal, essentially a large hole in the centre of my heart. The paediatric cardiologist saw me on 29 July. He told Peter and Angela of the diagnosis and that I would need open-heart surgery when I was about ten months old. This came as shock, upsetting them both and further extending the worries, uncertainties and unknowns associated with my heart condition.

Meanwhile, and of course being blissfully unaware of all this, I had started to recognise Peter and Angela. Now I was smiling a lot and had also discovered my hands, with which I could get and hold a small ball. I was mouthing my toys and, when they weren't in my mouth, I was talking and gurgling most of the time.

In August, Angela took me to Perth to meet my grandad, her father, and also her brothers and their families for the first time. My Aunty Sue, married to Angela's brother Jeff, remembers this visit very well. She writes: *Alicia visited us with her (then) foster mother, Angela ... Alicia was about three months old, and she instantly became part of our family, with her two cousins (David and Sam) sharing their prized toys with her every waking moment.*

On 13 September, some more good news. My physiotherapist said I was achieving all the normal developmental milestones, and then, as if to prove her right, I rolled over for the first time a few days later.

I'm not sure whether it was due to the chilly and dry Canberra climate, or my heart/lung condition, or a combination of both, but I was sick with colds and bronchitis on and off for the first eighteen months, with only brief periods of respite. At one stage, I was needing so much medicine that the kitchen bench looked like a pharmacy! Sometimes I saw the doctor several times in the same week, and I spent lengthy periods on antibiotics. All this was incredibly stressful and worrying for everyone, especially Angela who was caring for me full time (and, thirty-eight years later, still is) with many hours on her own while Peter was at work.

Late in September, my birth father, Neville, and Damian my older brother came to spend a few days with us so that they could see for themselves how I was progressing. Unbeknown to me or Damian, while they were with us, Australia II won the America's Cup against what seemed to have been impossible odds. Could this have been an omen for my life … winning through against huge odds?

The next big event was my legal adoption by Peter and Angela. This occurred on 23 November 1983, at the judges' chambers of the Supreme Court of the Australian Capital Territory. As part of the process, Peter and Angela both had to declare an affidavit to prove that they would be fit and proper parents, both in good health, and also able to provide me with a secure and loving home. To their immense joy, the adoption was approved, and, from that moment, they officially became my parents. Some days later, I received a new birth certificate including their names as my mother and father.

What is it?

And then, Christmas was upon us. This was a very special time … our first Christmas together. I don't remember anything about it, but I love the photo of me on the floor next to the nativity scene (which we still have and has been prominent at every Christmas since), being fascinated with an amazing Christmas tree and its flashing lights.

As we entered 1984, the time of my planned open-heart surgery was drawing ever closer, while I was continuing to slowly grow and put on weight in between bouts of colds or bronchitis. For growth and for weight gain, I was well below the lowest percentiles on the baby progress charts.

Then the big day arrived when Mum took me to Sydney to be checked by the specialist team in preparation for my surgery. But it was not to be. The doctors found that I already had very high pressures in my pulmonary artery

> *... my heart was inoperable, and my heart condition would have to be treated medically for the rest of my life.*

(between my heart and lungs) and closing off the heart valve would have been too dangerous, possibly causing heart failure. So, effectively, my heart was inoperable—with the medical knowledge available at that time—and my heart condition would have to be treated medically for the rest of my life. Mum and Dad were both very upset as they had hoped that surgery would resolve some of the underlying difficulties I was having and hopefully lead to a healthier and fuller life.

My First Birthday

A little while later, on 20 May 1984, I celebrated my first birthday. That morning, my mum came into my bedroom and said, almost sang: *It's your happy birthday!* This was caught on a video, but, unfortunately, the footage has been lost. My dad well remembers all the presents I received, fully covering an entire lounge chair and spilling over. There were lots of teddy bears. I was very spoilt, and everyone was so happy at the little party held in our home; somehow, despite all the uncertainty and struggles, I had made it through my first year, and everyone was keen to celebrate this.

Perhaps my first birthday did "rub off" on me because I have simply *loved* birthdays ever since. In fact, as soon as I have finished celebrating one birthday, I start looking forward to the next one, so Mum and Dad have asked me not to start talking about my birthdays until 1 May! (But I usually manage to raise the subject every few days nevertheless 😊.)

So, I finished my first year. Despite (or perhaps because of) my ongoing struggles in feeding, and the up and down nature of my health, I was basically a very happy and secure little person. I smiled a lot and enjoyed interacting with Mum and Dad, their friends and my toys, especially all those stuffed bears and dolls.

By then, I had also started my love affair with books. Mum and Dad remember one occasion when I was only a few months old. I was in my stroller while we were in a shopping centre, and I was holding a little cloth book open (like a small newspaper) with both hands, studying it very intently as we were moving along. This brought a lot of smiles from other shoppers who must have thought it was pretty cool.

Childhood Years

Some Very Important New Abilities

My wonderful support team was continuing to help me along. Apart from my paediatrician and paediatric cardiologist, I also had: an occupational therapist to help me with things like fine motor skills; a physiotherapist who assisted with exercises designed to improve my overall muscle tone (which was very low) and, therefore, my movement; and a speech therapist who, amongst other things, was helping me to learn how to chew. All these different therapy procedures and instructions mostly fell on Mum to implement with me, although Dad also helped when he was home. Of all these interventions, helping me to chew and swallow without gagging were the most important as these abilities could bring my problems with feeding to an end.

> *This was a major breakthrough and brought most of my feeding difficulties to an end.*

So, two important things happened when I was about eighteen months. Firstly, and after countless hours of Mum stimulating my cheeks—as instructed by the speech therapist—one day I surprised everyone by suddenly (finally!) chewing and swallowing. This was a major breakthrough for me and brought most of my feeding difficulties to an end. For the first time in my short

Woohhoo! I could finally enjoy my food!

life, I was actually able to keep most of my food and drink down. No one can imagine how much stress and angst this new ability took away from me and my parents about my feeding. Life for all of us, and especially Mum and me, became so much easier and therefore much more relaxed.

Then, not long after, I took my first steps and started walking. Yay! Now I would be free to roam and explore much more easily ... and quickly. Not that this made life easier for my parents 😊.

Welcome Changes from the Routine

As far as possible, given that I wasn't well for a lot of the time, we tried to do things together as a family that would be a break from the daily routine of Dad going to work, and Mum caring for me at home, or taking me to the various medical and other appointments. With my godparents living within walking distance of where we lived, we often strolled to their house on a Saturday or Sunday afternoon to hang out with them and their young family, sharing the latest news and developments about the children, and providing mutual support or advice when needed.

Another change from the routine that I thoroughly enjoyed from a very early age was any visit to a zoo or animal park. Any new animal that I saw for the first time fascinated me, and I was always eager to pat or touch them when possible.

While Canberra is quite a distance from any beach, we all relished opportunities to leave that rather cold and dry place to spend time on one of the fabulous beaches on the south coast of New South Wales, particularly around the Bateman's Bay area.

On almost a yearly basis, Grandad would come from Perth to spend a few weeks with us. During his stay, and when possible, Dad would take leave and we would all go on a short tour or holiday together to the south coast or to explore the Snowy Mountains near Cooma.

On the beach ...

With my grandad enjoying a day out.

I loved spending time with my grandad, and from the very first time he met me, he loved and accepted me without any qualms or reservations. I think he really enjoyed spending time with me as well. He always called me *darling*, and he was always very tender and caring with me.

Oma and Opa

Getting to know each other.

Just before I turned two, Oma and Opa came to visit us in our new house which we had built in Mackellar, then a new suburb in North Canberra. This was also their first opportunity to spend some time with me. At the start it was a bit awkward given their reaction to my being adopted by Peter and Angela. Well, I think I must have made a good impression and quickly put most of their fears and concerns about me to rest. After returning home to Brisbane, Oma sent us this extract from the book *The Clowns of God,* by Morris West, referring to a little Down's Syndrome girl:

> "I know what you are thinking, you need a sign. What better one could I give than to make this little one whole and new. I could do it, but I will not. I am the Lord and not a conjuror.
>
> "I gave this mite a gift I denied to all of you: 'Eternal Innocence'. To you she looks imperfect but to me she is flawless, like the bud that dies unopened, or the fledgling that falls from the nest to be devoured by the ants.
>
> "She will never offend me as all of you have done.
>
> "She will never pervert or destroy the work of my Father's hands.
>
> "She is necessary for you. She will evoke the kindness that will keep you human. Her infirmity will prompt you to gratitude for your own good fortune. More!
>
> "She'll remind you every day that I am who I am. My ways are not yours, and that the smallest dust mote whirling in darkest space does not fall out of my hand …

"I have chosen you; you have not chosen me. This little one is my sign to you, treasure her!"

Oma added this little note:

This passage I read, and it reflects so much of my thoughts, coming back from my visit with you. I am very grateful for those days, as I am so happy to see what a beautiful child Alicia is … these words [from the book] make you very still inside and I thought I had to pass this on to you both. I will keep my copy always.

This letter, which made my dad cry when he first read it, was dated 20 May 1985, my second birthday.

So, at only two years old, I had already achieved something very, very important … through meeting me, and getting to know *me*, rather than just focussing on my disabilities, the views of Peter's parents were completely turned upside down. From now on they would accept and love me dearly as their granddaughter, and, from now on, they would be **my** Oma and Opa.

> *So, at only two years old, I had already achieved something very important …*

(*Note by Dad:* While she is never aware of it, or orchestrates it in any way, Alicia's ability to melt hearts and evoke kindness from just about anyone she meets is one of her most precious and endearing gifts. As for Angela and me, Alicia has changed us in ways we cannot adequately put into words, other than the words quoted above: *She is necessary for you. She will evoke the kindness that will keep you human.*)

First School Experiences

After I turned three, I was enrolled at Cranleigh Special School serving North Canberra, the area where we lived. So my own little adventures into the wider world began. Of course, Mum kept a very careful watch on how I was coping and, from then on, for all of my school years, always kept in close contact with my teachers to share in the good news of my progress and to deal with any difficulties or issues as they arose.

Without exception (was I just lucky, or blessed, or was it because of my amazing personality?) I had great teachers throughout my schooling; they warmly cared about me, usually making special efforts to help me to learn, or to just fit in with my classmates. Sometimes, if one of my fellow students did something that upset me, I would need some help and encouragement not to get fixated on that situation or person and worry about it too much. This is something I would always need help with, and still do, to some degree.

Having fun at school

Once I became more familiar with my teachers, the other children, the school routine and its surroundings, I really enjoyed myself. I made friends quite easily and enjoyed learning, especially if it involved reading books and playing games. Sometimes, though, if I was feeling unwell or tired, Mum would get me at lunchtimes.

Then it was time for me to enter Year 1 at St Monica's Primary School in Evatt. This is a Catholic School. As it didn't have a special education unit to provide any extra support I might have needed, I was fully integrated into Year 1 with all the other students. Again, with the encouragement and support of my teacher, I made good and steady progress and was generally able to keep up with my classmates in these early primary years.

My Foster Brother

Were they crazy? As if caring for me was not enough (or was it because of what I had already taught them?), Mum and Dad felt that there was room for another child in our family, and so they explored the possibility of fostering. After going through all the formalities, Brenden came to live with us and stayed for two years from 1985 to 1987 before going back to his family to live with his grandmother. While it wasn't always easy having him with us (especially for Mum), I grew very fond of Brenden, and he really liked me as well. It was very quiet at our house when he left ... and we lost contact with him after that time, except for a brief visit and overnight stay with us in Perth some years later.

Some of my Favourite Pastimes

As a young child, I loved watching TV programs like *Sesame Street* and *Playschool*, and also enjoyed the TV series: *The Lion, the Witch and the Wardrobe*.

In 1989, fifty years after the original movie was made, *The Wizard of Oz* was released on video. Mum and Dad bought this for me, and from the first time I saw it, I was hooked! I watched it many times, and loved the story as well as each of the characters, except, of course, the Wicked Witch of the West. I quickly learned all the songs and knew the words by heart. My favourite song was "Ding Dong the Witch is Dead", because this wicked witch gave me the heebie-jeebies!

This movie remained a favourite for many years, and once for school fancy dress I dressed up as Dorothy and had a little toy dog—Toto—in a wicker basket. I won a prize for that costume.

From when I was still quite young, I have also loved stories and books, especially cookbooks. Bible stories were

Dorothy and Toto

> *I remember Alicia asking me if I had read the story of Easter and Jesus. I answered that I would read it. Alicia warned me: "It has a sad ending."*

another favourite. However, the story about Jesus being crucified really upset me, that people could be so cruel to someone who was so kind. So, each year as Good Friday approached, I would often become increasingly upset, and also didn't like going to the very sad and sombre church service on that day. Even looking forward to Easter Sunday and Easter eggs didn't change how I felt about Good Friday.

Apart from the children's bibles, the Narnia stories and the Goosebumps scary story collection were amongst my favourites. I especially liked the *Werewolf of Fever Swamp* in the Goosebumps series.

I also enjoyed listening to children's songs written by Peter Coombe, and some especially funny ones by Colin Buchanan, like "I Want My Mummy". I went to some of their live concerts with Mum. These were lots of fun and very enjoyable for me. Even Mum and Dad came to know many of these songs by heart, having heard them over, and over, and over 😊. Now, many years later, I can still remember most of the lyrics.

Daly River, Darwin

Before I turned seven, our family "walkabout" adventures had begun in earnest. Once again, I would have to ask if my parents were (are?) crazy!

In March 1990, we found ourselves in Daly River, an Aboriginal community in the Northern Territory. Why, do I hear you asking? Well, Mum and Dad had been thinking for some years that a change was needed, away from the daily grind of working and living in the somewhat bureaucratic "bubble" town of Canberra. Also, while I had been with them (or was it "because"?) they had both become strong and active Christians and increasingly felt a call towards any missionary work with the church, work which we could do as a family.

They discovered and then applied to an organisation (PALMS Australia) which specialises in placing ordinary Catholics and other Christians, with much needed skills and expertise, as volunteers in developing countries or in mission communities in remote areas of Australia. Placements are normally for at least two years and can be for singles and for families.

Of course, Mum and Dad were mostly thinking of coral beaches and palm trees associated with a possible placement in a Pacific island nation. However, God had other plans: we were destined for Daly River, about two hours southwest of Darwin in the Northern Territory.

There are very large crocs in this river! One of these was in the news on the day the decision was made to accept a placement there. Apparently a man had gone to the river at the back of the pub and was washing his head when the croc grabbed it and started to pull him into the river. The only way he escaped was by repeatedly poking the croc in the eyes. Very lucky. After we arrived there, someone pointed this man out to Dad, who noticed he had a big depression in his forehead where one of the croc's teeth had left its mark.

Another reason Mum and Dad felt that we could go on this adventure in this remote part of Australia was that the situation with my overall health and my disabilities had, by now, become known and was quite stable. When they asked my paediatrician about the possibility, he told them that it should be "OK", but he added: "Better sooner rather than later."

Just before leaving Canberra for Daly River, a reporter came to visit us at home and the newspaper article he wrote concludes with these words: *And Alicia, well she'll continue to be Alicia—bright eyed, full of life and love which makes Down's Syndrome children so special. "I think she will be the key ..." Peter said. "She is so accepting and brings love out of other people. People seem to mellow in her presence."* Nice one, Dad.

At Daly River, we lived fairly comfortably in a large permanent caravan (set up under a roof to keep the sun off) at a place called *The*

Five Mile. This was originally an emergency shelter for when the Daly River floods, allowing the community to move there temporarily with their vehicles to ensure continued road access to Adelaide River and to Darwin. However, when we lived and worked there, it was also an Alcohol Awareness and Family Recovery Centre for those struggling with substance abuse. Mum and Dad both worked as PALMS volunteers to run the facility, and we had family groups (both adults and children) of Indigenous Australians coming from all over the Territory to attend the four-week, live-in programs.

About to go to class at Daly River

Of course, many of them fell in love with me with my small frame, pale skin and lovely blond hair, all of which contrasted so strongly with them, mostly very dark skinned and with jet-black hair. One group of children from a community "just up the road", Port Keats (now called Wadeye) named me Kupilii … little bush rat! I also made a good friend with an older Aboriginal man, Jimmy Namatu, who played the didgeridoo and showed me how to play it … Well, I tried!

While we lived at The Five Mile, I went to the St Francis Xavier Catholic School in Daly River. This was, and still is, predominantly an Indigenous primary school with children from a number of different language groups gathered in this community. At that time, the principal of the school was Miriam Rose Ungunmerr Baumann, who was also a well-known Aboriginal artist.

After my initial adjustment to this very different environment, I settled in well and was readily accepted by my teachers and my fellow students, although sometimes there was a bit of teasing between all the students, which upset me. There was no special program for me but, being a small school with children of differing learning abilities and stages, it didn't matter. Unfortunately, from watching some of my classmates, I did learn some rather rude habits, like swearing and poking out my tongue.

One day, I wondered off into the bush and couldn't be found. Yes, this caused a major panic. Luckily, there was a group undergoing the program there, and all the Aboriginal women roused on their men to: *go and find that little girl!* With me was our dog Spotty, a stray who had wondered into The Five Mile one day, and, after much coaxing and cajoling, had become our pet. Anyway, Spotty was quickly spotted (excuse the pun) and then I was found in the long grass soon after. By then, I had somehow walked across a steel beam over a creek (dry, but the beam was high) near the bore pump. Much to the relief of Mum and Dad, and everyone else, I was soon back at our caravan.

Indigenous culture has some very respectful rules when people are yarning in a circle. How was I to know that you don't just go barging in? Well, on one occasion, I walked up to a group of women sitting in a circle, talking away in their language, and just squeezed in. Laughingly, they just made the circle a bit larger for me, made me feel very welcome and continued talking.

Mum, Dad and I were often invited to join in hunts for bush tucker: wild geese, long-neck turtles, flying fox and wallabies. These were always very enjoyable, and often filled with laughter … especially the time when Dad was wading up to his arm pits in a billabong in a line with other men trying to catch turtles hiding in the water grasses. After a while, a big pile of these grasses built up in front of him. Like the other men, Dad then threw this clump over his shoulder so he could move more freely. But with that clump, a sneaky turtle was sent flying high into the air. The women, seeing this from the bank, went into hysterics, shrieking with laughter.

After a while, Dad did manage to catch two long-neck turtles which were roasted over the fire that evening. They tasted a bit like chicken, but the fat sacks, which are considered a delicacy, were very rich.

Croc spotting on the Daly!

Sometimes the children staying with us at The Five Mile would build bush shelters, and I would be invited to join them. Skin colour didn't matter at all, and I always enjoyed these play and make-believe times. They also showed us how to identify the various palms and other plants, including water lilies, which are both safe and good to eat.

Although you may find this strange, we often swam in the Daly River, near the road crossing, and we all enjoyed this very welcome break from the heat and from the daily work routines. We quickly learnt that the local Aboriginal people knew where the crocs were. To be *extra sure*, Dad always made sure that there were other people between us and the deeper waters …

One of my absolute favourite stories of our time at Daly River is when, during the hot and humid build up to the wet season, we had a very large and loud thunderstorm one night which woke us all up. After Mum and Dad settled me down and reassured me that everything would be OK, we were all lying awake in our beds as the storm was slowly moving through. Then my terrible Dad sat up in bed very quietly in between lightning flashes and very carefully positioned himself with a scary face and grabbing hands poised over Mum. Then, when the next flash went off, Mum screamed out in terror as Dad was lit up, hovering above her like a ghost from a horror movie. Dad immediately dropped back on his side of the bed, dissolving in hysterical laughter, while Mum was repeatedly punching his shoulder and yelling at him. (He claims he still has the scars.)

In mid-1991, we sadly left Daly River and moved into our next temporary—and very mouldy—home at Anglicare in Winnellie,

Darwin. Mum and Dad were now helping (still as PALMS volunteers) a joint venture of the Anglican, Catholic and Uniting Churches, referred to as CAAPS (Council for Aboriginal Alcohol Program Services) to become incorporated and to build its first treatment and training facility at Knuckey's Lagoon.

> *Alicia's school has proved to be a real blessing and already she seems to be thriving ... with two hours per day of extra classroom assistance. She seems really happy, and we are noticing some real progress academically and socially ...*
>
> *Dad's diary*

Of course this meant another school change for me, now finding myself as a student at Holy Family Primary School. Coming from the small, mostly Indigenous school at Daly River into this much larger school was quite an adjustment. However, once again, I settled in quickly, again being blessed with a wonderful teacher and soon making some really nice friends. The school made me very welcome, and I was given support by a teaching assistant, as well as having access to occupational speech therapy once again. I was becoming very adaptable ... and resilient.

For me, the most memorable event while at Holy Family School was when we had to dress up for the Nativity play at Christmas. I was selected to be one of the angels, and Dad made me a huge set of wings, so large that I couldn't just walk straight through any doors but had to go through them sideways! Dad also made me a halo ... but it kept slipping ...

Alicia: a little angel but with big wings, with one of her friends

Back to Canberra

As 1991 slipped away into the New Year, our two-year commitment as PALMS volunteers was now quickly ending. Mum and Dad were trying to work out what the next stage of our life would be … to return to Canberra or to go to Perth to be near Grandad and Mum's brothers and their families. We knew that Grandad was becoming frailer, and, of his four adult children, Angela, my mum, was the only one who he would listen to in relation to his ongoing care situation.

So, big decisions needed to be made in these first few months of 1992. Originally, Mum and Dad had been willing to spend longer on mission with PALMS, but now it seemed better for us as a family to move on after our two-year term was completed. After many lengthy discussions—of which I was mostly ignorant—they decided that the ultimate goal would be to move to Perth, but that first we needed to return to our home in Canberra for a time to organise ourselves and plan such a big move across Australia.

Consequently, in early April, and after a four-week holiday in a small campervan driving down the east coast, we arrived in Canberra, just as it was starting to become *very cold*. Actually, the change from a tropical climate was too much for me and, not many weeks later, I was badly ill in hospital with pneumonia. This was a very scary time for me, and for Mum and Dad, although I tried to be very brave. The nurses in the hospital were very kind and, with the care I was receiving, I was soon back to my reasonably healthy self.

I was now back at my old school, St Monica's, but certainly not the same person I was before we went to Daly River. Not only older, but also my unique personality was now emerging much more strongly. I had developed a very good sense of humour and sense of fun, often making my family and friends laugh at the things I said or did, like hiding in the cupboard to try to get to Narnia (*The Lion, the Witch and the Wardrobe* was still one of my very favourite books and movies).

> *[A memory] ... I have is sitting in the back of the car somewhere near the Glass Mountains. I was feeling car sick and Alicia was trying to make me feel better by rubbing my face, supporting my chin up close and kissing my cheeks. She was so concerned. This empathy she has for others is pretty special.*
>
> *This mixed-up world needs more people like you, Alicia: full of empathy, happy with yourself, trying to make others happy, and with a great sense of fun.*
>
> *Aunty Yvonne*

Another of my "special ways"—which was already clear by then—is that I have always been very sensitive to others being upset in any way. Dad thinks that I know if he is having a bad day before he does! From my earliest years, I have always tried to comfort others if I they seem sad or are hurting in any way; this instinctively comes straight from my heart. At the same time, since I was very young I have been able to sense whether other people are accepting of me just as I am, and, if they are, well I just love that, and respond accordingly ... also from my heart.

With the support of my favourite teacher, I was prepared for the Sacraments of Reconciliation and Holy Communion, which occurred on 2 December 1992, and 21 February 1993. Mum and Dad bought a beautiful dress for my First Communion, and I looked very pretty for this very special and happy occasion. It felt so good to wear such a lovely dress and it made me feel just ... can't think of the right word. I also received some very nice gifts, and my good friend Annie, who made her First Communion at the same time, gave me a special book called *Our Church*. I cherish memories such as these.

With Dad in my First Communion dress

As we entered 1993, Mum and Dad were preparing for our move to Perth. By then, our house had been on the market for a couple of months, and Dad had been actively looking for jobs. But nothing was happening, even though we were all praying hard. Grandad's health was steadily deteriorating, so something just had to give. Then Mum and Dad decided that we would make the move regardless and not wait any longer. Finding a job and selling the house would have to be done from Perth. Incredibly, on the very next day after they made that decision, we received an offer on the house, and a phone call confirming a job offer for Dad in Perth! Is that the result of "stepping out in faith"?

Our Life in Perth

So, in March 1993, we said goodbye to Canberra and set off on our four-day drive to Perth. I was fine for the first two days, but then it really dawned on me that we were, once again, going a very long way from my school, my friends, my home in Canberra. This time, however, I began to realise that we *weren't* coming back. So, I became very, very sad and cried while we were driving across the Nullarbor. It took Mum and Dad a long time to cheer me up; and it upset them as well.

But I didn't stay sad for long, because when we arrived in Perth, we were warmly welcomed and fully embraced by Mum's brothers and their young families. We had visited them a few times from Canberra and once from Darwin (for Christmas), but this time we would be staying near them, with no plans to move again in the foreseeable future. So, we had many family visits over the next months, and we often spent time with my grandad, usually several times per week.

These family times were most enjoyable. Some of my best and favourite memories were when I was painting with my Aunty Yvonne; getting together with all the families at Christmas; visiting my cousins and playing with them; and my birthday parties, especially the time when one of my silly, tall cousins placed lots of pointy party hats on his head!

While we were in Perth, I went to St Denis Catholic School at Joondanna. I don't remember too much about this school except that I made some very good friends and, when they came to my birthday party at our home in Leederville, we played "wrap the mummy" by winding rolls of toilet paper around each other. We also had a lot of fun sitting together in Dad's large hammock slung in the trees at the back of our yard.

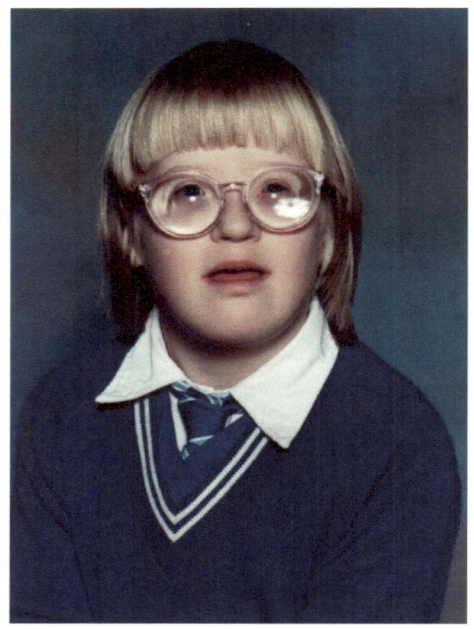

My school photo when I was about eleven years old

I was happy at St Denis and always tried very hard at whatever I was asked to do. I pushed things a bit too hard at a swimming carnival, though, and had to be rescued by one of the teachers when I just ran out of puff. While this really frightened Mum and Dad, they were also very proud of me for "having a go" to the best of my ability. I still won a ribbon.

Often on the weekends, in the mornings before it became too hot, we would go to one of the little beaches close to the city. I really enjoyed these times, playing in the rock pools, climbing on the rocks, and walking out onto some of the reef at low tide looking for fish and other sea creatures.

My first holiday diary (and there have been quite a few since) was for our long trip north along the Western Australian coast to Coral Bay and Monkey Mia where I fed the dolphins. The water there was very, very cold, and our legs were turning blue while we were trying to feed the dolphins darting around us. One afternoon, while playing along the beach at Coral Bay, I slipped and fell into the water.

Being so cold, it took my breath away and I sort of froze face down in the water. Luckily, Dad saw it all and rushed in to lift me out. I was frightened, and when I could breathe again I started to cry. I was fine, but it certainly reminded Mum and Dad that I needed to be watched very closely.

(Of course, when it comes to me, Mum has almost always been like Radar in that TV show: *Mash*. She knows exactly what I am doing … from several rooms away!)

Life in Leederville was good. The church was just around the corner. We could see the steeple from our back yard, and always heard the bell ringing very clearly. On Sundays after Mass, we often indulged ourselves at one of the local cafés (my favourite was called *Fat Bellies*) for coffee and cake.

We usually walked to church on Sundays, except if it was raining. Then, one day, as we were walking up the slight hill on the way to church, I had an episode, collapsed and couldn't continue. This was alarming for all of us, and I was off to the doctors as soon as an appointment could be made. We discovered that the weakness of my heart had suddenly progressed so that from now on I would only be able to walk quite short distances (about fifty metres) and would need a wheelchair for anything longer. Even before this, I was walking quite slowly and, for longer distances, Dad would have to carry me by giving me a piggy-back.

> *The weakness of my heart had suddenly progressed so that from now on I would only be able to walk quite short distances (about fifty metres) and would need a wheelchair for anything longer.*

Having to use a wheelchair was a major turning point, but I didn't let it get me down, and nor did Mum and Dad. Actually, we quickly found it to be very helpful and, for the first time, could take *very* long walks as a family easily and comfortably. Our favourite was to walk right around beautiful Lake Monger, seeing all the black swans, especially when their eggs were hatching, and then, a few weeks later, seeing the little cygnets running around.

During these months, my grandad—who had, by then, been diagnosed with Progressive Supra Nuclear Palsy (PSP)—was steadily getting worse. PSP is a rare brain disorder that causes serious problems with walking, balance and eye movements, and, later, with swallowing. Sadly, we saw all these symptoms slowly becoming more apparent, severely affecting every aspect of his life. Yet he always still called me *darling* and was always very happy when we came to visit. He never complained about his situation although his life was steadily becoming increasingly difficult. Probably because he never complained, or became grumpy, he was a real favourite and very popular with the staff at St Michael's Nursing Home in North Perth.

> *The one memory of Alicia that has always stayed in my mind is from her grandad's (Angela's father) funeral in 1994. Alicia was not quite eleven years of age, but she was so supportive to her family and, in particular, towards her nine older cousins, patting them on their backs and saying: "It's okay!"*
>
> *Aunty Gail*

Very sadly, my grandad died on 25 February 1994, less than a year after we moved to Perth. Fortunately, we had many enjoyable and memorable times together during those months, and they were all very, very precious. None of this would have been possible if we had remained in Canberra.

I was very sad, crying, but also very brave at Grandad's funeral. Unfortunately, the priest had got his days and times mixed up and didn't appear for the funeral service, so Dad led the service instead.

(*Note by Dad*: The hearse and all those attending were patiently waiting outside the chapel when it eventually became obvious that the priest wasn't coming. Having planned most of the service with Angela, I was familiar with it and so volunteered to lead Grandad's funeral. It wasn't easy given my own grief and emotions, not to mention the lack of any prior experience. Nevertheless, it all went to plan, and after we had sent Grandad off with "Anchors Aweigh"—he was a Royal Navy veteran—family and friends said that it was a lovely service.)

I really missed my grandad and felt sad for a long time after his funeral.

Welcoming my grandad at Canberra airport

He was such a kind and gentle man. From when I was very young, I always loved being with him.

At about this time, I got a new pet, a jet-black American spaniel called Loni. She was a lovely dog and companion for me, although she was very shy and took a while to warm to anyone. Before she came to live with us she had been a breeding dog

Sharing a cuddle with Loni

and had had several litters. So she wasn't really used to having lots of love and affection from us humans. It was good to have a pet again, and I loved cuddling with Loni, which I did … a lot.

Previously, we had a very playful cocker spaniel called *Monty*, and a kitty named *Tiger* … a tiger only by name. They had already been with Mum and Dad for a few years when I arrived on the scene. When we went to Daly River, some of our good friends kindly agreed to adopt Monty and Tiger. We were all very sad to say goodbye to them. Mum cried when we had to leave Monty. Although we saw them again when we returned to Canberra, everyone agreed that it would be too disruptive for them to come back to us. They were both very well cared for and happy in their new families. So, after settling down in Canberra, we visited a pet shop and found a delightful kitten for me. I named her *Sally*.

So, life continued on routinely and without any significant dramas into and through 1995. I was making satisfactory progress at school, although by now, in upper primary, the work was much harder for me. I could read and write fairly well, but subjects like maths and working with money were very difficult. Of course, I very much enjoyed having money to spend—and still do—but I just can't work out how much change I should expect. Luckily, most shopkeepers are honest and don't try to take advantage, and I always have Mum or Dad or another supportive adult with me when I am shopping.

The various doctors and specialists were happy with my progress and my generally stable health.

Life was good, and I always enjoyed spending time with my cousins, aunties and uncles whenever the opportunity arose, which was quite often.

> *I want everyone to know how much I love my family.*

But then, as we were approaching the end of 1995, and unbeknown to me, another major change was in the wind. The directors of the company in which Dad was working as a consultant had asked him if he would be interested in opening and running an office in another capital city in Australia. If it was a successful venture, he would be invited to join them as another shareholder and director. Of course, this sparked many long conversations between Mum and Dad, and another period of uncertainty and potential upheaval.

As a family, we were very happy in Perth, and life was very good for all of us, but then the challenges and potential opportunities associated with developing a business in another city were also very attractive to Dad, and unlikely to be offered again. There were so many issues and factors to be carefully weighed. Brisbane quickly became the preferred city to consider because Dad's family was based there and it would give them an opportunity to get to know me better over an extended period, not just on lightning visits for brief holidays.

Another consideration was that in 1996 I would become a teenager and start high school; so a school change was inevitable in any case.

In the end, after many days (and restless nights) the decision was made. We would make the move to Brisbane in early 1996. When we told our Perth families, my Aunty Yvonne said only two words: *Oh poop!*

Teenager ...

Into High School ... and a Surprise for Dad

One of the reasons Dad left the Army was so that we could have a more settled life as a family! Well, now I found myself in Brisbane in yet another different home and environment. It was my fifth home in six years: Daly River, Darwin, Canberra, Perth and now The Gap, a suburb of Brisbane. Luckily for all of us, I was really quite adaptable. Or was this something that I just had to become?

Once we had found our new home in The Gap, Mum and Dad's next challenge was to find a suitable high school for me. After many enquiries, I was enrolled at Mt Maria Secondary College in Mitchelton which had a support unit for students with disabilities. This was, and still is, a Catholic school in the Marist tradition, and, amazingly, the principal was a Marist Brother who had taught my dad science when he was in high school at Marist Brothers Rosalie.

Dad tells a horrible story, which I love to hear over and over (and just has to be in my book!) about being taught biology by the same brother who now, many years later, was the principal of my new school. Rosalie wasn't a rich school, and when it came to having specimens for dissection in biology lessons, there just weren't any available. Not to be discouraged in any way, this enterprising young brother noticed a dead cat by the side of the road when he was out walking one morning and immediately grabbed it for his next biology lesson. Well, this was arranged in the laundry under the brother's house, and what followed was a very gross dissection of the poor animal. Judging by its condition, it had obviously been hit by a vehicle sometime during the previous night. It was also deep into *rigor mortis* so that its legs had to be wrenched apart to allow the dissection to go ahead.

The experience was enough to cause nightmares. Not all of Dad's classmates stayed for the full dissection experience, especially when a probe into the cat's bladder caused it to empty itself by spraying some of the boys standing near its rear end. To cap it off, when they all returned to the classroom for the next lesson—religion—taught by the same brother, it wasn't long before the good brother started chewing his fingernails!

But that was then …

Within a few weeks of starting at Mt Maria, I became a teenager. One of the best parts of being at my new school was that I quickly made really good friends with a group of girls, all my age, some of whom I am still in touch with all these years later. We thoroughly enjoyed each other's company and always had a lot of fun together. From the start, they came to my birthday parties (which I somehow manage to have every year!). On one occasion, Mum and Dad organised a great treasure hunt which everyone really enjoyed, and then we played party games like musical chairs, pass the parcel, pin the tail on the donkey, and squeak piggy squeak, which had us all in hysterics.

Live Theatre and Musicals

In 1997, Mum and Dad took me to see *Phantom of the Opera,* starring Rob Guest and Danielle Everett, at the Lyric Theatre in Brisbane. This was my first live stage show and I was absolutely spellbound and engrossed, on the edge of my seat for much of the performance. Where we were sitting, the chandelier was right above us, and when it fell down and swung, I wasn't scared but very, very excited. I loved it all, and since then *Phantom* has remained one of my favourite musicals. I now know all the lyrics of the songs by heart, and love all of these beautiful and haunting melodies.

*My little joke ... with **those** socks from the Wicked Witch on my legs!'*

That was just the beginning. In the following year, we all went to Sydney to see an amazing performance of the *Lion King*. While living in Brisbane we also enjoyed *HMS Pinafore*, *Chitty Chitty Bang Bang*, *Annie*, *Shout*, *Singing in the Rain*, *Beauty and the Beast* and *Les Miserables*. Then later, after we had moved (again!) to Ravenshoe in Far North Queensland, we saw *Phantom of the Opera* (twice) and *Wicked* in Cairns, and also travelled back to Brisbane to experience *The Wizard of Oz*. When in Sydney in 2013, we saw *South Pacific* at the Sydney Opera House.

So, as you can see, I became (and still am) quite a culture buff ... and it all started in 1997 with *Phantom*. In all these shows, I have enjoyed the acting, the special effects and staging, and, above all, when there was inspiring or moving music and lyrics. One of the songs

Before the show

> *I became (and still am) quite a culture buff...*

which always makes me laugh every time I hear it is "Master of the House" from *Les Miserables*. My all-time favourite song from these musicals is "The Point of No Return" in the *Phantom* because the performance by Rob Guest and Danielle Everett was incredible and deeply moving when I first saw and heard it. From that time till today, I have loved this song; it takes me back to that first live performance.

Another School

I remained at Mt Maria till I was part of the way through Year 10 in 1998, when it was decided that I would move to Aspley Special School for my final years of high school. The main reason for the change was that years 11 and 12 at Mt Maria would be at a different campus which was not accessible for someone like me with my physical disabilities. Mum and Dad and my teachers also felt that I would benefit from the extra support and help that was available at Aspley. At first, I was very sad about having to leave Mt Maria, and especially my wonderful friends. I was very fond of them as we had developed such a good understanding and "vibe" together.

One of the things that I clearly remember of this new school is that, soon after I arrived, we had a Student Commonwealth Games competition to coincide with the real games being held in Kuala Lumpur. I was very happy to win one silver medal for bocce, and two bronze medals for netball and basketball. Another very happy memory is going on school camp for several days at Rocky Creek near Landsborough. A real highlight for me was when we were spotlighting after dark one evening and my torch lit up a mother possum with a baby on her back. This was a very exciting discovery for all of us.

As I moved through the last years of high school at Aspley, more emphasis was being placed on what I (and my peers) might do after Year 12. So the school arranged for us to attend Tertiary and Further Education (TAFE) courses in hospitality at Southbank in Brisbane, and also organised various work experience placements. The ones I remember were at the Queensland University of Technology restaurant and at Able Care, an organisation supporting people with disabilities.

As a result of these courses and work placements, it became clear that I would have difficulties in understanding numbers as well as sequential instructions and work processes involved in most forms of work. Also, my stamina, and thus my ability to stay on a task, was limited. Consequently, future opportunities for a meaningful job would be few.

> *I remember my Year 12 graduation ceremony very well. It was a very special night.*

Under a special arrangement, I was able to stay at Aspley Special School until the end of 2001, when I had already turned eighteen. I remember my Year 12 graduation ceremony very well. It was a very special night. I looked lovely in my new dress which was especially made for this big milestone in my life, and I had my hair up and beautifully curled. Mum and Dad, some of my aunties, uncles and my cousins, and some of my school friends from Mt Maria were there for the celebration dinner. What a wonderful night. I felt so proud and happy.

With Mum and Dad on my Year 12 Graduation Night

University

But what to do now that school had finished?

Fortunately, there was another possibility for me. I was selected to take part in a special computer and literacy program called *Latch On* at the Queensland University in St Lucia, Brisbane. So, I was off to uni!

This program would run over two years, 2002–3, for two days per week. Poor Mum had to drive me there and back each day, about forty-five minutes each way from where we lived. Lucky that we "girls" now had a hot little red car …

At that time, Latch On was still a pilot program aiming to provide opportunities for young adults like me to continue our literacy development after secondary school. Another objective was to help me build confidence in using computer technology to increase my ability to read and write. Above all, the program was designed to promote my sense of independence and possibly increase any work placement opportunities.

While at Latch On, I met a nice boy who used to call me "pussy cat" and once gave me a little peck on my cheek. *Ooooh lala!* Here I also made other good friends, and we shared lots of laughs during our time together. One special memory I have is that, for my nineteenth birthday, Mum made cappuccino brownies for me to take to uni so that I could celebrate with my friends and the staff.

At the end of my first year, Mum, Dad and I attended the graduation ceremony. I was thrilled that Simon Black from the Brisbane Lions was the guest of honour. He was a very handsome young man. From that day on I have always been a huge fan of the Brisbane Lions … and of Simon Black.

All too soon, the time for me to finish the Latch On program was rapidly approaching. For my final project, I made a big PowerPoint presentation called *Walks in the Park* which was the story of my time at Latch On. Then it was my turn to graduate at the end of 2003, and, yes, there was another Lions footballer, Luke Power, as our guest of honour. I was very happy to celebrate my graduation, and Mum and Dad were very proud of me for what I had achieved during those two years.

As a result, I am still very confident in using computer technologies, things like iPads, mobile phones and PCs. My favourite application is Facebook so that I can keep in touch with all the latest news about my family and friends.

Socialising

When not at uni, I spent some time with *Hand* , an organisation supporting people with disabilities. This was a very social group, and we did a lot of fun things together. Having a very sweet tooth, I especially looked forward to baking goodies … which we did most weeks. There were also good opportunities for participating in arts and crafts. One of the things I made was a toilet roll holder which I still use in my "facility".

(*Note by Dad:* Angela and I are often in stitches over what Alicia comes out with, and her use of "facility" was another such occasion.)

Snorkelling … on the Reef

In May 2003, we flew to Cairns for my cousin's wedding, and, before that, for a brief holiday in Port Douglas. One of the best experiences of this short holiday was the day trip to Swallow Reef on the *Aristocat*. This was my first visit to our wonderful Barrier Reef and, having taught myself how to snorkel in our pool at home in Brisbane, I did an amazing snorkel (helped by a flotation board) with one of the snorkelling instructors. It was magnificent, so much to take in, but I was most excited when I saw a parrot fish and a giant clam. Afterwards, I received a PADI "Champion Snorkeller" Certificate and was very proud of my achievement.

During our time at Port Douglas, I turned twenty (yes, I was spoilt as usual) but, more importantly, we did a day trip to the Atherton Tablelands in our hire car. We didn't know it at the time, but that day trip was to sow the seed for our next big adventure. Mum and Dad were very impressed with both the beauty and the liveable climate of the Atherton Tablelands, and they quickly started to think: "What if?" …

Our "Tree Change" ... and Other Great Adventures

The Big Move

Then, as soon as we returned to Brisbane, Mum was on the computer searching for suitable properties on the Atherton Tablelands.

(*Note by Dad:* For the length of our stay in Brisbane, I continued to lead the Queensland office of the IT consulting company that I joined in Perth. In 2001, a much larger company bought this national business. So, by the middle of 2004, I would complete my three-year obligation to stay on after the company was bought out. If we were going to make a substantial change, now would be the time to do it. I also need to record that the demands and stresses on all of us of my running a small consulting business had been unrelenting since we moved to Brisbane in 1996. It was high time we all stepped away from this "pressure cooker".)

One property that really appealed to Mum and Dad when they saw it advertised on the internet was near Ravenshoe (on the southern end and highest part of the Atherton Tablelands). The house was situated on a one-acre, rural-residential block with well-established gardens, and with an adjoining easement to the Millstream River. Only Dad flew up to inspect it. He reported that it had a *good feel, and that he thought we could make a go of it*. So, the deal was done and, early in August 2004, I found myself with Mum and Dad at the front gate to our new property, with the removal truck about half an hour away. That was the first time Mum saw the place and, very lucky for Dad, she agreed that we could indeed *make a go of it* there.

Still, for all of us, it was another big upheaval, especially after spending eight plus years comfortably settled in Brisbane and familiar with the various support services that I needed so that I could get out and about, interacting with people other than my parents, much as I love them. Now all these arrangements needed to be put in place anew. When Mum started to make enquiries—even before we moved from Brisbane—it quickly became clear that there were no suitable support organisations for people with disabilities in Ravenshoe, the nearest being in Atherton, about 50 km away.

Nevertheless, arrangements were soon made with a disability support organisation for my new support workers who would help me to get out and do some of the fun things I like: visits to libraries, shopping and having treats or meals at cafés and restaurants. We had to manage these schedules carefully because of the extra time and costs involved in travelling when we couldn't find any support workers based in Ravenshoe, which was most of the time.

> *I always felt very good about these "jobs" of mine.*

Early on, we also met one of our immediate neighbours, who ran the then Eagles Nest Wildlife Hospital, taking care of orphaned and injured animals. I enjoyed visiting and holding the little orphaned wallabies once they were big enough to hop around. For several years, I sponsored some of the animals at Eagles Nest, helping to cover the costs of their care. I was very happy doing this. In fact, I considered this to be one of my "jobs". Another was to sponsor Guide Dog puppies to help with the costs of raising and training them. I always felt very good about these "jobs" of mine.

We also explored the surrounding countryside and were delighted to discover a beautiful swimming hole on the Millstream, about one kilometre from our house. In the first years, when vehicle access via a bush track was reasonable, we often went swimming there. However, as a result of cyclones (we experienced two of these, "Larry" and "Yasi") and heavy wet seasons, the track was scoured out, became very rough and so much harder to negotiate, even for a four-wheel drive vehicle. So then I didn't swim there very much, although Dad sometimes walked down for a swim.

Our new lives in tropical North Queensland were starting to take shape.

Horse Riding

Very soon after our arrival in Ravenshoe, Dad began taking me to North Queensland Riding for the Disabled (RDA). This sparked my love affair with horses and riding that was to last for thirteen years. With the continual support of my wonderful coach, I soon became very comfortable on the gentle horses that were available. My favourites included: Judo, who was my first horse and one that I rode for several years; Atlas (although he used to fart a lot); and Potsy. A

My first hug with Apache

few years later, Mum and Dad bought Apache for RDA so that I could ride him. Apache was a leopard appaloosa gelding, about nine years old when he was bought in December 2009. This would be my main horse for my remaining years with RDA and we became very good friends. He loved it whenever I bought carrots, apples or sugar cubes for him to enjoy.

When we had horse sports and gymkhanas, I won a bunch of ribbons, including a first prize for dressage. For some years, I spent two days each week at RDA, one morning for the RDA riding program with other riders, and the other one-on-one for most of the day with my coach, who also became one of my support workers in the latter years of my riding career. I really love her. She is still a good friend, and I was sad when she had to return to South Africa so that she could look after her mother. But I well understand how important this is, for family to care for one another, no matter what the cost.

My Busy Life

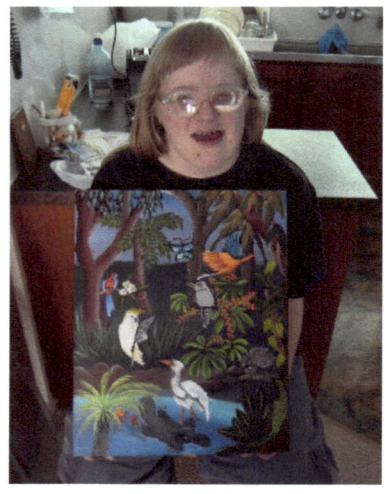

One of my art works ... with a little help!

Another regular activity that I really enjoyed was art, made even more special with the wonderful support and help of one of the local artists in Ravenshoe who also ran a lovely gift shop. So, on Wednesday mornings for many years, I created many folk-art paintings, many of which were given away to family and friends. In the end, we ran out of wall space in our own house, so then I decorated little gift boxes, various place mats, serving trays and similar items. Most of these were given away as gifts, but even now, years later, I still have quite a collection at home.

Often, I was spoilt with little gifts or freebies from the shopkeepers and that always made me feel special.

Over time, I came to know many people in Ravenshoe, mostly from when I was in town with Mum or Dad or with one of my support workers. I also became very well known, was very well accepted, and always felt safe. Often, I was spoilt with little gifts or freebies from the shopkeepers and that always made me feel special. I also developed my own "Babes' Club" of special (mostly young, but not always) women who I really liked because of their outgoing, warm personalities, and because they welcomed and accepted me just as I am; and they still do. Now my "Babes' Club" is Australia wide and also includes quite a few cousins 😊.

I settled in very well into this great little community, so much so that from shortly after we arrived, I was very comfortable with going on one of the floats (for St Barnabas Anglican Church) in the annual Ravenshoe Torimba Festival. And I did this for a few years …

With the Ice Queen on the Lion, the Witch and the Wardrobe float

before I became a bit shier and therefore more reserved.

On the days when I wasn't busy (and at this time, I was really quite busy: riding on Mondays; in Atherton with my support worker on Tuesdays; art on Wednesdays, in Ravenshoe; riding and horsey time on Thursdays at RDA) I enjoyed just being in my room, listening to my audio books, watching DVDs, doing some more art, or just relaxing reading one of my books. From early on, I was, and still am, quite independent and self-contained, keeping myself busy doing things that I enjoy.

One of the wonderful things about living in this rural residential area was the wildlife which came to visit on most days. We had a bird feeder right outside one of our loungeroom windows, and during the daytime it was a very popular attraction for rainbow lorikeets, pale-headed lorikeets, red-winged parrots, willy wagtails, pigeons, doves and so on. After dark, we often found one or two possums sitting in the feeder munching away, and it wasn't unusual to have some very cute rock wallabies and betongs, as well as bandicoots (not so cute because of the paralysis ticks they carry) underneath the feeder, picking up the scraps.

Expanding my Horizons

New Zealand

Chilling at the Antartic Centre—Minus 8C!

So our years in Ravenshoe rolled on. But we didn't spend all our time there. We had some awesome holidays and other trips.

In 2006, we spent a month in New Zealand touring parts of the North and South Islands. For me the highlights of this trip were: the Māori village in Rotorua, learning about their culture and experiencing their vibrant singing and dancing; the amazing glow worms in the Raukuri cave, in Waitomo; snorkelling with the dolphins off Kaikoura (Dad did the snorkelling, I stayed on the boat with Mum); and the visit by Dad and me to the Antarctic Centre in Christchurch, where I saw some little blue penguins and went on a Hagglund ride. At Queenstown, Dad and I went on the Skyline Gondola right up to the top of the mountain. However, I didn't like the ride or getting too close to the edge of the viewing platform at the top. It was all too high for me.

Our stay in Queenstown marked the end of a magnificent holiday.

The Outback

In June the following year, we explored the vast Gulf Savannah region as far west as Karumba in the Gulf of Carpentaria, then returning to the east coast and driving all the way to Cooktown. Little did I know that in the years ahead we would all become much more familiar with the Gulf Savannah area … but that story is for later. One of the highlights for me was going fishing in the Gulf on the charter boat *Kerry D*. I caught two bream and two grunters, but, sadly, they were all too small so had to be put back in the water. Dad caught a decent-sized bream which we cooked for dinner that night with some lovely mud crab, also caught while on our charter.

On the rockpile with Mum and our guide

Another new adventure for me on this trip was to go fossicking for gems at O'Brien's Creek, near Mt Surprise. I found several pieces of topaz and later had them polished.

East Timor (Timor-Leste)

Then in 2010 we were off for a very big adventure to East Timor, another overseas trip, but this one would be very different!

(*Note by Dad:* From 2001, our family had been involved in several humanitarian programs through the church and also through PALMS Australia, yes, the same organisation through which we had been placed as volunteers at Daly River a decade earlier. By 2010, I had completed several trips to East Timor in support of these programs. This visit was another opportunity to check up on their progress, and, where needed, try to push them along a bit. The people of East Timor—despite their mostly abject poverty and complete lack of resources and facilities we take for granted—always greatly inspired me by their sheer joy of life, and the importance they placed on their families. This visit was to be the first time that Angela and Alicia would travel with me to experience these amazingly resilient people, their culture and the very difficult circumstances which confronted them daily. Taking Alicia into this developing country with so few medical resources in case anything went wrong was not without risks, but it was an adventure that, as a family, we just couldn't pass up.)

On 4 July 2010, only a few days before we left for East Timor, Dad was ordained, at St Monica's Cathedral, as a permanent deacon in the Diocese of Cairns. This was a very big occasion for the three of us, and we were joined by a large group of family and friends, from near and far. I really enjoyed the celebrations before and after and was very proud of Dad.

Then we were off to Dili, via an overnight stop in Darwin and a very early departure the following morning. Our first few days were spent at Gleno orphanage in the mountains behind Dili. Supporting this orphanage was one of the projects my family was involved with through a foundation that Dad and a few of his Army friends had set up. I really enjoyed meeting some of the orphans, the PALMS volunteers working in Gleno, and a group of donors also staying at the orphanage at the same time. We had a lot of fun together over those three days.

Then we returned to Dili, and while there we visited Ahisaun, an organisation supporting people with disabilities. In East Timor, people like me, who have disabilities, are mostly hidden away by their families in shame, and are given no opportunities to develop their *abilities*. Ahisaun's main purpose was to show and prove to the whole community that it needn't be like this. This was another project both the foundation and PALMS were supporting.

> *In East Timor, people like me, who have disabilities, are mostly hidden away by their families in shame, and are given no opportunities to develop their abilities*

Wearing the tais we had each been presented with and listening to "You Raise Me Up"—very emotional.

When we arrived at Ahisaun, we were treated like honoured guests. The whole community was gathered and welcomed us with songs. Then one young man who was crippled and couldn't stand up or walk except on his knees, sang "You Raise Me Up" in English, which caused us all to shed tears. This visit was deeply moving and very inspiring for all of us, especially seeing the courage and hope of these young people, despite their sometimes quite severe disabilities and the level of societal indifference—and even prejudice—they were striving to overcome.

Other visits while we were in East Timor included Atauro Island and Atabae. Our trip to Atauro was on a small rib boat and had been arranged by one of Dad's Army friends serving in East Timor because the regular ferry wasn't due to leave for a few days. While this crossing started off smoothly, before long the wind blew up and I felt like we were in a washing machine, being tossed around by the waves. I was fine, though, just hanging on for dear life as we all got completely drenched by the spray. After what seemed like many hours, we were very happy to enter the calmer waters around Atauro.

On arrival, we met another PALMS volunteer who had decided to stay in East Timor after his voluntary placement and who, by then, had a young family. He had set up an eco-resort on the island, not to make a profit but to provide funds to send young East Timorese to university.

We stayed with them for a few days, living in one of the grass huts, and it was a most enjoyable time. It was like being in a paradise, peaceful and tranquil, the main sounds being the wind in the palms, and the gentle lap of the waves on the shore. Dad particularly enjoyed snorkelling on the magnificent reef, easily accessible from the shore. All too soon, however, it was time to leave. Our return trip to Dili was on the ferry, a much more peaceful and calmer ride but shared with many other people as well as assorted pigs and chickens (some of the poor pigs were trussed up on poles).

Then, to complete our trip, we spent some days in Atabae, a community Dad had visited several times since 2001, and where a number of humanitarian projects were being undertaken through the church and through PALMS. While Dad was having some meetings about these projects, Mum and I visited one of the nearby villages with one of the health workers being trained by PALMS. Then we visited one of the schools, and all the children came to meet me and have their photo taken. I felt really good about this.

With the children at Atabae school

After just over two weeks in East Timor, we returned home, and this is what Dad recorded in my trip diary for me: "I enjoyed East Timor, meeting lots of nice people, making some new friends, seeing the pussycats (there were quite a few that visited with us during our stay in Atabae) and seeing some of the projects that my family has been supporting. Maybe I could go back there someday. I will pray for the people that I met, especially I would like to pray for the children."

Hopefully, in our own little way, we gave them a real and present witness to the fact that someone with a disability—and his/her family—can still lead a happy and fulfilling life. That is what I was thinking as we strolled along.

Dad

(*Note by Dad:* Alicia did incredibly well during this trip, especially considering the unrelenting heat and humidity associated with being so close to the equator, and the lack of any air conditioning in all the places we stayed. She adapted exceptionally well to each different place, situation and persons she met, and—Angela and I are sure—also left a lasting and very positive impression behind. I distinctly remember when we were walking to a nearby restaurant in Dili one evening pushing Alicia in her wheelchair. So many people in the street stopped to look at us, probably for them a most unusual sight. Hopefully, in our own little way, we gave them a real and present witness to the fact that someone with a disability—and his/her family—can still lead a happy and fulfilling life. That is what I was thinking as we strolled along.)

Fiji

What seems incredible now is that within a month of returning home from East Timor, we were travelling overseas again, this time to Fiji for a planned holiday with some of our good friends. The contrast with East Timor could not be greater ... from basic living in grass huts to four- or five-star resort accommodation, with luxurious facilities and air conditioning.

Dad and I coming in to land.

But then, would you believe it, I found myself back in a grass hut ... on Castaway Island. This was also a very nice resort which became the setting for one of my greatest adventures yet, very risky and undertaken without Mum's prior approval! Dad and I had been jet skiing (one of my favourite activities—I have a need for SPEED) and were relaxing in the shade of the palm trees when we noticed that parasailing was starting close to where we were sitting. After watching a few people take off and come back with great big smiles on their faces, I turned to Dad and told him that I wanted to do it. This greatly surprised him as I don't normally like heights. So, after he had repeatedly checked with me that I was certain, Dad bought the tickets and away we went, harnessed together in a tandem rig. Well, I really enjoyed this … it was just wonderful and thrilling to be soaring through the air over the ocean, although we did descend a little too close when the boat turned. We landed safely if somewhat awkwardly, but now with big smiles on *our* faces, and then went to tell Mum, who had been peacefully sleeping in our hut, blissfully unaware. She was shocked and surprised … but Dad didn't get into *too* much trouble.

On a slightly less adventurous and risky note, by now I was generally comfortable enough to ride horses other than Apache and often took an opportunity to do so when we were on holidays. So, while we were at Castaway Resort, I also rode one of their horses along the beach. While not as adrenalin rushing as parasailing or jet-skiing, I still felt good about myself, and empowered, in taking a risk by riding a strange horse in a completely different setting. My riding coach was always delighted when I told her about these escapades.

The Dinosaur Trail

Our trip to Fiji, especially so soon after East Timor, satisfied and quietened the "travel bug" for a while, but then, in June 2012, Dad turned sixty, and, to mark this birthday, it was decided that we would do the *Dinosaur Trail* in central Queensland. We all thought that this was a suitable choice of holiday for this significant milestone in his life as it would allow him to hang out with some other fossils 😊.

I thought this trip was incredible. I especially loved *The Age of Dinosaurs* display near Winton where I had my photo taken with Banjo, who looked like a velociraptor from *Jurassic Park*. Here we could also see the very careful way in which the fossils were being worked to separate them from the surrounding rock without being damaged. Other highlights of this trip were: the *Dinosaur Stampede* where I could see the actual footprints that various dinosaurs made some ninety million years ago—this is a number I cannot even imagine; and *Kronosaurus Corner* in Richmond, which had amazing fossils of huge sea creatures from when much of Australia was under water, a vast inland sea.

Fossicking for fossils ... where's Dad?

While in Richmond, Dad and I went fossicking for fossils (apart from the one who was with me) in one of the large quarries near town. We split the layered rocks and found many tiny fossils of marine creatures, including some tiny fish, which hadn't seen the light of day in some hundred million years. This was just such good fun, and even a little addictive. I didn't want to finish our "dig" and would have been happy staying there for many more hours to see what we could find.

So, with my adventurous parents, my horizons were not only being expanded in *space* (through our travels to some very different and interesting countries and places), but also now in *time*, by our trek along the *Dinosaur Trail*, seeing firsthand the evidence of life flourishing on earth all those millions of years ago. This fascinating experience helped to kindle my interest in archaeology and ancient civilisations, but more about this later.

My Thirtieth Birthday Holiday

Then in the following year, 2013, it was my turn for a big milestone birthday. I was turning thirty! Now I know that for most people thirtieth birthdays are considered significant milestones. For me, however, thirty years was given as my maximum life expectancy by one of the doctors who Peter and Angela spoke to on the day that I was coming into their care. So, of course, we all wanted to celebrate this birthday of mine in a very special way, and that is exactly what we did. A big part of our joy in my turning thirty is that my health had been very stable for some time, and that the doctor would be proven quite wrong.

As well as having a big party for me at our home in Ravenshoe, we had decided to take most of the rest of 2013 off from other commitments and take a holiday around Australia. And this is exactly what we did … in our caravan which Mum and Dad had bought just for this purpose in late 2012. Yes, we had been planning this for quite a few months.

With my Aunty Kiki and her painting

My big party was held on 18 May, with a small crowd (about forty in all) of family and friends all very happy to celebrate with me. A huge surprise was when my Aunty Kiki arrived. She had made a special trip from Brisbane, and I was so very happy to see her, giving her a great big hug. Aunty Kiki had completed a beautiful painting of my horse

Apache for my birthday, and I was very touched and happy to receive this lovely gift.

> Alicia's thirtieth birthday is a significant memory of mine.
>
> At the time, Alicia had a pony called Apache, and I had done a painting of him for her thirtieth birthday. As a special surprise, I travelled to Ravenshoe from Brisbane so that I could attend her party. But it was all kept as a big secret! I stayed with my sister Brigitte and her husband in Cairns and, on the big day, the three of us drove to Peter, Angela and Alicia's home.
>
> As the car pulled up, Alicia saw my sister and her husband but hadn't seen me yet. When she spotted me, we both burst into tears, and later, when presents were unwrapped, Alicia was so happy with the painting. It was such a well-kept surprise ... which reminds me of another story Peter and Angela told of one Christmas morning. In the very early hours, Alicia had unwrapped every present under the tree while they were still sleeping.
>
> **Aunty Kiki**

A local lady made a wonderful, layered chocolate mud cake, all decorated with white chocolate, covered in horseshoes, also in white chocolate (my favourite). What a cake it was! What a memorable afternoon! It rained heavily at one point but that didn't dampen the mood of the party, especially when a good friend of mine started pretending he was Elvis by crooning some of his well-known songs, which I thought was hilarious.

Two days later, with the caravan all packed, we said goodbye to our home in Ravenshoe. We would not return for more than six months. It was very hard for me to leave my dog Peaches, but we felt that she would be well cared for by our house sitter, and she was.

During this long holiday, my "room" was at the back of the van, really just my bed with a concertina door that I could pull shut for privacy. I called this space my "chicken coop" because, really, it wasn't that much bigger; in fact, I have seen much larger chicken coops! Nevertheless, I soon settled into our travelling routine where we would mostly drive for a day or two, and then have a few days in each place to explore and enjoy the sights and attractions of interest. When we stopped, Dad would often put up the annex (if it wasn't too hot) so that we all had extra room in which to spread out and find some extra personal space.

It would be too much and potentially quite boring to tell the story of our trip in detail, but for me the real highlights were these:

- Finding the fascinating "Lost City" (near Lake Crawford in the Northern Territory) in one of the travel books, which then convinced Mum and Dad to change our planned route so we could go there. As it turned out, we flew into The Lost City by helicopter on Dad's birthday, which made it extra special. That night, we had dinner at the hotel—*Heartbreak Hotel*— a most suitable name because that night Queensland lost a State of Origin game.

  A selfie by Dad of the three of us in the chopper

- Visiting Katherine Gorge and doing a boat tour through this incredible place.
- Coming out of ICU in Darwin Hospital ... yes, you read this correctly. Shortly after leaving Katherine, I became sick with a fever and a very bad cough, both of which are not easy to manage on the road in remote parts of Australia. When we arrived in Kununurra in Western Australia a day or so later, Mum and Dad took me to the hospital in the evening for a check-up. It was decided that I would be evacuated to Darwin Hospital by the Flying Doctor. Mum went with me, while Dad stayed behind. Yes, and he was freaking out!

- I was admitted to the ICU as I was very sick. Dad arrived by plane the next evening, and for the next six days Mum and Dad alternated in keeping overnight vigils by my bedside. But with the great care of the amazing ICU team, I got through, and then I was well enough to be discharged … to everyone's great relief. Dad wrote this about me in his trip diary:

"Throughout these difficult and draining days, I was deeply moved by Alicia's incredible spirit and resilience. Even when very ill, she still welcomed the doctors and nurses into her little 'world' defined by her bed and all the surrounding monitoring equipment. She kept a special place in her heart for all her nurse 'babes', particularly those who were pregnant."

- Visiting El Questro a few days after coming out of hospital, and having a ride on Moonshine, named because he was a rescue horse found injured and alone somewhere out in the nearby bush on a moonlit night.
- Flying over the magnificent Bungle Bungles, and other incredible landscapes in the vicinity, in a sea plane, and, on our way back to Kununurra, stopping on an island in Lake Argyle for afternoon tea.
- Riding a camel at sunset on Cable Beach in Broome, and, a few days later, when deep-water fishing, catching a huge Spanish mackerel. My diary included the following note: *Feeling great again!*

What an amazing experience; me leading followed by Mum and then Dad

- Paying for Dad to snorkel with the whale sharks in Exmouth. I was so happy to do this for him, and he was just so excited to have such an amazing, once-in-a-lifetime experience. (*Note by Dad:* it was an incredible day. We snorkelled with several different whale sharks. Being so close and swimming alongside these very gentle giants, just cruising along with a slow side-to-side motion of their huge tail fins, was an unforgettable experience. For us snorkellers, however, it needed rapid, high energy kicking with our fins just to keep up. What made the day even more special was that on the way out to where the whale sharks were expected to be, the spotter plane saw a humpback whale and a calf. So the boat dropped us in the water right along their path. The mother looked me right in the eye as she passed by, and that brief connection will always remain a very special memory. What a wonderful gift from Alicia to have these experiences.)

- Enjoying two more birthday parties for me in Perth, with my aunties, uncles and cousins. I was very spoilt, and it was very special for me to celebrate my thirtieth with them as well. So, that made three birthday parties in one year, just for little old me. All of my extended families are always very kind to me, and this makes me feel very good about myself. Have I mentioned before how much I love them all as well?
- Seeing the *Secrets of the Afterlife*, a display at the museum explaining how the Ancient Egyptians understood, and prepared for, life after death. It included a display of a *Book of the Dead*. I had already been interested in Ancient Egypt for some time, and so I found this display fascinating, as did Mum and Dad, and Aunty Gail, Uncle Ron and cousin Simone who were with us. Uncle Ron kindly organised this wonderful afternoon for all of us.
- Checking out Riding for the Disabled in Perth, which was located quite close to the caravan park we were staying in. Luckily for me, I was able to ride Teno, a very pretty Haflinger pony.
- Going to Hahndorf (near Adelaide) where Dad bought a *Bum Burner*, a very hot German sausage which Mum took back to the caravan … in her handbag!

- Visiting Penola in South Australia, the place where St Mary Mackillop set up the first of her schools run by her order, the Sisters of St Joseph. St Mary really inspires me because she cared enough for isolated and poor children to try and give them a good education in order to give them more opportunities in life.
- Seeing my godparents in Canberra and spending time with my brother Damian in Sydney. This was really the first time that Damian and I were able to enjoy each other's company as adults. I love him very much and we both cherished these days.

With my brother, Damian; feeling very happy!

- Going to the Opera House to see *South Pacific*. I loved all the singing and dancing and thought that Stewpot was a "crazy twit". Another favourite character was Bloody Mary, wonderfully played by Christine Anu.
- Riding Bella the Clydesdale at *Barcoo's Barn* near Bathurst and seeing the Clydesdale and horse-drawn carriage display in conjunction with the Farmer's Market a few days later.
- My dolphin encounter at *Sea World* ... Dad was with me, but I had a one-on-one encounter with Coen, one of the incredibly well-trained dolphins. He did all sorts of tricks and also let me feed and tickle him. Even now, nearly

Hugs with Coen

nine years later, I still enjoy watching the DVD of that very, very special experience.

So, after just over six months on the road, we came back to our home in Ravenshoe. At first, it was very strange being back in a home which couldn't move. However, we all soon adjusted back to "normal life" and doing cool things like riding my horse, Apache. I had really missed him while I was away, so it was good to be back in the saddle at least once per week, and also to see my riding coach who I really like. Life mostly settled back to our normal routines, and I resumed regular outings with my support workers who I had missed while we were away.

Special Pastoral Assistant

One of the regular commitments for my family, which immediately resumed after we returned home from this long holiday, was to visit individuals and families in what is known as the Gulf Savannah Parish. After Dad's ordination in 2010, the Bishop of Cairns asked him to minister in this vast parish, some 1,000 km east to west, and between 200 and 400 km north to south. This part of Australia is very sparsely populated, mostly consisting of sprawling cattle stations, and some small towns scattered across the region.

(*Note by Dad:* Even before Alicia's thirtieth birthday holiday, the entire region was struggling through the joint impact of the Global Financial Crisis, live export ban, and widespread wildfires in late 2012, followed by drought. So we went out together several times per year while the drought continued (from early 2013 till 2019) to visit families on their stations. We also organised and delivered care packs, all kindly donated by very generous people and parishes.)

I am always a little reserved when meeting new people, and so I found our first visits, to each new person or family, a little confronting. However, I soon relaxed as each visit progressed and, over time, made many friends. On the occasions when Dad went by himself, he was often asked: *Where is Alicia? Why didn't you bring her?* Dad came to realise (he is a bit slow) that I played a very important part in these pastoral visits, even thinking that perhaps all that people expected *him* to do was to be my driver!

Seriously, though, I think that my presence (and personality) had a deep impact on many of the people who were so desperately struggling to keep their grazing businesses and livelihoods afloat during what were some very dark times, when even the country itself looked absolutely worn out and withered, when hope was hard to come by. So, when Dad was discussing all this with the bishop during a meeting, it was felt that my own role in these station visits should be recognised.

Then, not many days later, on 18 July 2014, a letter arrived for me in the mail from the bishop:

> Dear Alicia,
>
> Greetings from your Bishop!
>
> It is my great pleasure to offer you an honorary position with the Diocese of Cairns as a Special Pastoral Assistant because of your important role in supporting the people of the Gulf Savannah Parish.
>
> Alicia, you have already been visiting the Parish for about 3 years and have formed caring relationships with many people, both in the communities and on the stations. In doing so, you have demonstrated that you are a key member of our pastoral team …
>
> I hope, therefore, that you will accept the position of Special Pastoral Assistant to recognise the valuable contribution you are making to the Gulf Savannah Parish and to our Diocese. May God bless you in this important pastoral role.
>
> Yours truly in Christ,
>
> +**James Foley**
>
> BISHOP OF CAIRNS

Well, when I read this, I just burst into tears. I was just so happy, and of course I accepted the invitation which also recognised the work I had already been doing with my parents. A few days later, there was another envelope in the mail for me, this time with my badge: *Special Pastoral Assistant*.

For the next few years, I always wore this badge very proudly whenever we were visiting station families in the Gulf Savannah. With some of these individuals and families, we developed lasting friendships.

Sadly, in more recent times, I have not really had much energy or stamina for this role. As a family we now tend to visit the Gulf Savannah for only a week or two in the dry season when temperatures are not so extreme. At other times, Dad goes out on his own, which is not ideal but nevertheless important to maintain the connections which have been established with so many people.

We also try to take advantage of annual events such as rodeos, shows and festivals to meet up with the people we have come to know. It is always good to see them again and catch up with all the news while enjoying events like horse sports, bull rides, and dog trials.

A Slower Pace ... but with Big Interests

Health

Since 2013, when I became so sick and ended up in Darwin ICU, my health has been quite stable. (Before that, I only had three other stays in hospital, twice for pneumonia and once to have my tonsils removed; so I have been very fortunate given my underlying health issues.) Nevertheless, I still have to be very careful with any respiratory illnesses, especially flu and, as this section is being written, COVID, which is now spreading through the community.

So, for nearly nine years, there haven't been any visits to hospital for me. Of course, I am still under the care of a cardiologist and thoracic specialist who both keep an eye on me. However, I only need to see them once or twice per year. Overall, my health has been reasonable, and I have been able to do most of the things that I wanted to do.

On the other hand, now I don't have the stamina or inclination to be as active as I used to be. A few years ago, I had outside activities for nearly three full days per week. These have now reduced to two half-days per week, and that is all I can reasonably manage. I do get quite tired and am more than happy just to be at home to do my own thing. My room is my castle, and I have always managed to keep myself quite busy.

Perhaps it is also because I am getting a little bit older and am very content with my life at home, and being with my silly parents, who I sometimes refer to as my "alien and inconsiderate parents" 😊.

Support Workers and NDIS

Over nearly twenty years, I have had a number of support workers, most recently funded through the National Disability Insurance Scheme (NDIS). With them I have thoroughly enjoyed sharing morning teas and lunches at various cafés and restaurants; looking at shops, especially newsagents; exploring the libraries in our area; and, sometimes, going on special excursions.

> *Without exception, I become very attached to my workers, and they become attached to me.*

I become very attached to my workers and they to me. I look forward to spending time with them and doing things together. This hasn't always been recognised by some of the disability organisations supplying my workers in that they seem to think that, if my worker is not available for any reason, then any other worker will do. Maybe for them, but not for me …

For that reason, under NDIS, I recruit and manage my workers directly with the help of an organisation that does all the paperwork and accounting for NDIS. This is an excellent arrangement and helps me to keep the workers that I want to have. It is also very flexible if things need to alter from time to time.

I have been truly blessed with my support workers over the years. With only one or two exceptions they have been very special people in my life, always very kind and caring. They have greatly added to my overall quality of life. I am mostly very happy when I am with them unless I am feeling tired; then it can be all a bit too much to be out and about with them on that particular day.

My "Ologies"

I know this is a funny title, but it does indicate how many areas I am very interested in and, with many visits to the libraries and also watching documentaries, are subjects I have taught myself a great deal about. I find all of these fascinating, and I love cross-referencing similar information between my books, and also between my books and any DVDs or documentaries on TV. Dad says I have an incredible memory, and I often really surprise him with how easily I can find specific information in even quite large books.

I love learning about these favourite subjects, and I don't need any outside motivation; I am quite motivated myself.

> *I like learning new things and studying new information. I have an inquiring mind.*

Egyptology

Egyptology is my all-time favourite subject. I am fascinated by everything this ancient civilisation achieved over more than three thousand years. I love learning about the pharaohs, kings and queens, particularly the female ones, like Nefertiti, Nefatari (wife of Rameses the Great), Cleopatra, and famous pharaohs like Rameses, Tutankhamen and Akhenaten. Their tombs and the way they were decorated are amazing. I really like the hieroglyphics and art works which showed incredible skills.

I also love learning about, and seeing, some of the everyday items that the ancient Egyptians used, like jewellery and gold, ointments and other beauty products used by the women.

I have a good collection of reference books in my own little library. Some of these I have found in second-hand bookshops and in Vinnies and Lifeline shops. My wonderful family and friends have also bought some lovely books for me.

To decorate my Egyptian "space" I have a ceramic bust of Tutankhamen in my bedroom and also two papyrus paintings hanging on the wall in the little alcove next to my bedroom door.

I keep as up to date as possible by looking out for relevant documentaries, and also as a subscriber to the *Ancient Egypt* magazine which is published in the United Kingdom. This gives me all the latest news about new finds and digs. Interestingly, my interest in

Ancient Egypt has also inspired Mum and Dad, who have learnt a great deal about this amazing civilisation through me.

Archaeology

I have also become very keen to learn more about other archaeological sites and discoveries around the world.

> *I like to learn about what people in the past have done and what they achieved and built; how clever they were. For example the Khmers built that amazing temple. And how other civilisations were so clever and industrious ….*
> *I would love to work on a dig site somewhere.*

One of my personal favourites is Angkor Wat in Cambodia. I think it is fascinating because of the way this large temple is built and the lovely architecture of each of the structures. Mum, Dad and I watched an amazing DVD recently about how the sun comes up exactly on the top of the main temple at the equinox. I would really love to visit Cambodia and learn about this remarkable architectural site and learn more about the Khmer people and their civilisation.

I also like learning about the archaeology of ancient Greece, and have been fascinated by the Terracotta Army discovered in China, especially how each of these warriors has a different face, and also by the sheer numbers and scale of this buried army,

Marine Biology

Ever since I was very young, I have always enjoyed going on a boat and have even snorkelled on the Great Barrier Reef near Port Douglas. Any opportunities to go on a glass-bottom-boat tour or

Enjoying a reef cruise in a semi-submersible

in a semi-submersible—so I can experience our magnificent marine life firsthand—have been seized upon. This has created my deep and lasting interest in marine biology. Over the years, I have studied a large number of books from various libraries, and also some that I have bought for myself. These are large reference books with photos and brief descriptions of an immense variety of marine life.

I can easily find many sea creatures and types of coral. Often my amazing memory helps me to identify particular fish and other creatures very easily.

Meteorology: Severe Weather

For some years, I was a member of the Australian Severe Weather Association, or, should I say, storm chasers. I wasn't able to chase storms myself, but I enjoyed seeing the antics of this group in chasing severe thunderstorms. I especially liked the photos and videos they shared online.

Closely related to this I like watching DVDs of the even crazier storm chasers in the United States, those who get as close as possible to large tornados. Not for me, but the strength of these storms fascinates me.

When we have a thunderstorm nearby, I usually watch it through my bedroom window, but when it gets too loud and too close, I run to Mum!

One of my own crazy and funny moments was when we were in our caravan at the Gold Coast during my thirtieth-birthday holiday. A massive storm suddenly blew up and threatened to rip off the awning. So my very silly dad went outside and hung onto it for dear life, while the storm raged on, threatening to take him to Oz, like Dorothy. Mum and I were watching horrified from the window. Dad says that our eyes were like saucers

Dad did save the awning, and afterwards we all laughed about what any of our camping neighbours might have seen or thought.

Now: Life is Good, and it is Good to be Me!

Now we are approaching the end of this story, so I would like to share some thoughts about my life now, as I am experiencing it in 2021–2.

Family and Friends

I very much like being me. I have been told many times that I am very kind and caring, especially for my family and friends who are all very special to me (have I said that before?). When there are opportunities to be with those who are dear to me, I really look forward to them, counting down the days if not the hours. Through Facebook, I always keep a very careful watch on who is having a birthday and will always make sure that Mum or Dad are aware of these.

So happy together ... with Brendan (L) and Damian

When it comes to my brothers, Damian and Brendan—and their partners, Angus and Caitlyn, respectively—they all hold a very special place in my heart. It has been one of my great joys in recent years to deeply connect with my brothers for the first time in our lives. I am proud of having a part to play in starting this whole thing by painstakingly writing a letter to each of them. In this letter, I told them how much I cared for them and how much I would like to see them more often. Since then, and together with Mum and

Dad and my brothers' partners, we have shared many very happy times, and I think this will now always continue. That thought makes me very, very happy.

At Christmas 2019, with (left to right) Brendan and Caitlyn, Angus (Damian's partner), my cousin Richard and Damian. I was so happy being together like this.

One of the special things I like to do is to give some of my family and friends some quirky nicknames. Here is a little list, and those who know … will know who they are 😊.

Aunty Kiki Wiki (she calls me her Blueberry Muffin!),
Aunty Chop Suey,
Uncle Jeffrey Bean,
Sheaney Weenie,
Cream Puff,
Bunty George,
Uncle Maladjusted, and
Aunty Bruschetta.

Being Kind to Each Other

I really don't like hurting people's feelings, and if I do something wrong that upsets others, I usually try to apologise. Sometimes, when I am feeling particularly tired, I can get a bit grumpy and withdrawn, not wanting to engage with anyone else. It's not personal; it's just how I am feeling at the time. Then I hope that people understand that I am not at my best and will give me some understanding and space. When I feel like this, I often feel bad later that I may not have been the nice person that I always like to be.

I am often surprised by the kindness of people I barely know, or even that of complete strangers. It is by no means unusual that someone will come up to me in the street and tell me how lovely my hair looks, or comment on how nicely I am dressed. In the shops, or at a café or restaurant, I am often given a little gift or offered a treat. These acts of kindness always make me feel very good.

(*Note by Dad:* One of Alicia's most endearing gifts is her own capacity to make people feel good about themselves, by just saying something nice to them or in some other way, such as expressing concern and compassion if someone seems sad or overburdened in some way. It is heart-warming to see this gift in action, as it is when she herself is being blessed in a similar way by the presence and kindness of others.)

Of course, I would like everyone to be kind and respectful towards others. I hate it when people are acting in cruel or disrespectful ways; I just don't understand why they would be like this.

Looking Good

With Mum's help and support, I have a very nice wardrobe with some very colourful outfits that I can mix and match. I like to look good when I am out; although Dad is not allowed to make any comments, even nice ones. Twice a year, before my birthday and just before Christmas, I have my hair coloured. I really look forward to having this done, and then love to share my latest looks with my family and friends on Facebook. I always receive a large number of "likes" and some very nice comments.

Keeping Busy

I enjoy going to the shops and have become quite an adept bargain hunter. I have a good understanding of prices and enjoy finding good deals, especially for books on subjects that interest me. Of course, shopping is tiring for anyone, let alone me, so I also love recharging my batteries with a nice treat at a favourite café or restaurant. If going for coffee and cake, or a meal, with Mum and Dad, I love to "shout" by paying from my own account.

However, while this chapter is being written, COVID is spreading rapidly through the community across Queensland. Consequently, Mum, Dad and I are spending more time at home and avoiding crowds and gatherings until we can assess what our "new normal" in a COVID-affected world might look like. So, for now, I am not able to do some of the things I really like … but then I am not alone. Nevertheless, we are doing some "COVID-safe" trips in our car, going to picnic areas or similar and enjoying this wonderful and very beautiful region of Australia.

When at home, I mostly keep myself very busy: anything from watching a movie or documentary, to doing some artwork (diamond dots being my latest interest), especially when I am making gifts for others. I enjoy spending time on my Nintendo Switch playing Mario games. I also like to read and to listen to story books on my CD player. In keeping myself occupied, I have been quite independent from an early age; rarely, if ever, do I feel bored.

I really love my little cat, Elvira; in fact, so much that it is hard to put into words. She is a lovely and gentle companion for me, and always makes me laugh with her antics. She usually sleeps on my bed at night and always lets me cuddle her for quite a long time before she starts to wiggle and wants to be put down.

With my COVID cat, Elvira. I love her to bits!

My Bucket List

Yes, I do have real hopes and dreams about my future, and I have my own little bucket list as well! Here it is:

1. Get a good-looking boy friend 😊
2. Go on an archaeology dig
3. Visit Angkor Wat
4. Visit Egypt
5. See my brothers more often
6. Go horse riding again
7. Spend time with all of my family as much as possible
8. More adventures …

I am not sure that all of these will be possible. Travel to other countries has always been a challenge because of my underlying health issues and the risks associated with falling ill overseas where the level of medical care I might need is less certain. Now, of course, with COVID, overseas travel is even more risky. But, hey, it is good to have things to dream about and to hope for, isn't it? It makes life interesting and worthwhile.

Closer to home, however, we are always looking for little adventures we can do together, like:

Cooking our favourite stir fry

Hooning about on the water ... the faster the better!

Enjoying the wildlife, up close and personal

Riding in a helicopter over one of the cattle stations—what you can't see is that there was no door next to me!

My Favourite Song

While I like many songs and styles of music, my all-time favourite song is from *Camp Rock*. I can really identify with the lyrics of this amazing song. In fact, I wonder if it wasn't written for someone just like me. Here is the chorus I like so much:

> This is real
> This is me
> I'm exactly where I'm supposed to be now
> Gonna let the light shine on me
> Now I've found who I am
> There's no way to hold it in
> No more hiding who I wanna be
> This is me

Do you like it too?

Stories by Family and Friends

While writing this book, Dad invited my family and friends to share any favourite stories or memories of the times we have had together. So this is what they said, or shared, in no particular order. I really appreciate that my family has expressed these lovely thoughts and feelings about me.

Aunty Bruschetta and Uncle Mally Mal

Alicia, from the day you were born, you brought a beautiful light to all our lives as a special place was made for you with Angela and Peter, two very remarkable parents who have provided an incredible life's journey for you so far. As you near your thirty-ninth birthday, and reflecting upon the beautiful woman you have become, the words that come to mind are: a generous spirit, gentle, kind and a hilarious sense of humour. A young woman strong in her convictions, but most of all, you have an incredible love of family.

The birth of a new niece or nephew has always given you a great sense of belonging, where you can join in with cuddles, hugs and words of encouragement. This is family.

You love life and any type of celebration with family, especially when it comes to birthdays. We have all been very blessed in so many ways in celebrating with you over the years and I hear the groan from mum and dad when you start planning your next birthday, and the current year's birthday has literally just been celebrated. This is a contagious excitement we all catch from you and laugh about…often

We are fortunate to have quite a number of artworks completed by you, Alicia. I especially love the gorgeous frogs you gave me, who chat to me in the kitchen every day.

A very talented young lady in all manner of art and craft, you are very passionate and also love to explore and read about the world around you. You enjoy sitting and sharing with us your love of horses and fascination with Egypt.

You are the World's Best Niece (WBN). We love you dearly and you hold a very special place in our hearts.

Uncle Jeffrey Bean, and Aunty Chop Suey

We are very proud as Alicia's uncle and aunt, especially with the names she gave us so many years ago, Uncle Jeffrey Bean and Aunty Chop Suey. Although there seemed to be no rhyme or reason behind us adopting these names, they have stuck fast.

When we were living in Manjimup, in the south-west of Western Australia, Alicia visited us with her then foster mother, Angela, and her much loved Grandad. Alicia was about three months old, and she instantly became part of our family, with her two cousins sharing their prized toys with her every waking hour.

Sharing a meal with Alicia has been a firm favourite. Not just actually sharing the meal at one of our homes or a favourite restaurant, but enjoying the stories of her birthday cakes and those of her friends and family whilst we have been living on opposite sides of the continent. Chocolate. Chocolate. And more chocolate.

So many special lunches prepared at our family homes with Alicia's help in the kitchen, and also at restaurants from North Beach (Perth) to Cairns, and in between. There was always a laugh with Alicia when she has had to, so often, tell her father to, "Behave, Peter!" Of course we all agreed: "Behave, Peter!" Then there was the time she actually gave up her wheelchair for Peter who was pretending to have had too many Hop Hogs. Angela, ever so patiently, with a kindly smile on her face, standing back watching it all happen and then a laugh, "Behave Peter!"

Alicia's love of Egyptology has fascinated us, and we have always been on the lookout for things for her to read and do. We lost her in amongst the old books at a second-hand shop when we were visiting. Nothing needed to be bought, but so much to see and enjoy. Our friends gave her a papyrus paper painting, knowing she would love it and research the story behind the painting. On a later visit, we saw how it had been framed and was on display in her bedroom along with her other treasured possessions.

When we think of our first trip to Cairns, we remember the café she picked for breakfast, the many walks along the foreshore, the ride down the Kuranda Sky rail, and Alicia pointing out her highlights on the drives around the region and, of course, stops at the best foodie stops. We were sure to take notice of the places we needed to visit. She is the best tour guide ever.

Aunty Yvonne

I am very happy to contribute to Alicia's story.

I immediately think about Alicia asking me, when she was still quite young, if I had read the story of Easter and Jesus. I answered that I would read it. Then Alicia warned me, "It has a sad ending."

Then there was the day in the car in Perth on our way to buy Wendy's Ice cream. Alicia told me that Tom (her make believe son) was to stay in the car. Sally (her make believe daughter) was allowed to come with us. However, I wasn't allowed to tell her mum because Angela thought they had both "left home". I still remember Alicia putting her hand on my lips to get me to keep the secret.

Most of my memories of Alicia growing up are her being happy, caring and full of fun. She always showed buckets full of empathy when she interacted with my mother, and always gave generous hugs.

Painting with my Aunty Yvonne

Whenever we were together, she asked how all her boy cousins (my four sons) were and wanted to know what they were doing. I also remember how fond she was of her grandad and how kind and gentle she was with him

Her happiness is on full display when she giggles and puts her hand over her mouth to stop laughing.

I well remember her love of cooking and still have her recipe book, full of chocolate treats. Her love of books has been a constant since she was very, very young, and her reading me stories from the bible is another of my fondest memories.

One of my greatest joys is when she brings Peter into line when he is being silly. "He is a pain", has been repeated many times.

Once, while sitting in the back of the car somewhere near the Glass House Mountains, I was feeling car sick. Alicia was trying to make me feel better by rubbing my face, supporting my chin up close and kissing my cheeks! She was so concerned. This empathy she has for others is pretty special!

This mixed-up world needs more people like Alicia; full of empathy, happy with herself, trying to make others happy, and with a great sense of fun.

Aunty Gail

From the moment Alicia came into the family she has always been shining like a bright light!

Alicia was a happy, bubbly and cheerful young girl and continued to be the same as she became an adult.

Alicia has always been a very loving and loveable person. As a youngster, Alicia always had a soft spot for her cousins!

Alicia's compassion for others is immeasurable.

The one memory of Alicia that has always stayed in my mind is from her grandad's funeral in 1994 at Karrakatta Cemetery, Perth. Alicia was not quite eleven years of age, but she was so supportive to her family and, in particular, towards her nine older cousins, patting them on their backs and saying, "It's okay!"

She was just incredible and seemed much older than her eleven years.

Love you, Alicia.

Cousin Jade

If I had to sum up my cousin, Alicia, in a few words I'd choose: caring, generous, adventurous and funny. Alicia is always ready with a hug and to help someone in need. She cares for all around her—her family, her friends, her community and nature. She's always ready to try new things and explore new places. Her adventurous spirit is inspiring and contagious. Plus her wicked sense of humour makes her so much fun to be around.

Love you lots, Cous. Don't you ever change.

Aunty Kiki

Now almost forty years of age, and considering that Alicia had many health challenges when she was born, she has grown into the most gorgeous woman. Through all the years, Alicia's beautiful inner spirit was always shining through.

With her family, Alicia has lived in many different places, and she has acquired Peter's sense of adventure x2.

In recent years, Alicia has also developed strong relationships with her two biological brothers, Damian and Brendan, a development which has been very special for all of them. We have had so many fun times with her and Peter and Angela. I know that she is having the best that life has to offer.

I love her to bits.

Damian—my brother

The day we found out we had a sister ...

On a Brisbane day—many years ago—two little boys named Damian and Brendan were sitting, anxiously waiting on a leather lounge out the back of a house. Mum had something she needed to talk to us about. Something that would change our lives and family forever. "Alicia is your sister," Mum told us. Our world exploded with excitement ... finding out we had a middle sister was the best news. This news of our sister Alicia made visiting her as little kids all the more special.

I love my brothers ... Damian (L) and Brendan

A fond early memory of Brendan's is Alicia's lava cake explosion at her birthday party. The cake poured out with chocolate, a fair amount finding its way onto the birthday girl's face. Luckily, the lava cake explosion did not deter her excitement of cakes. Fingers crossed someone in the family has a photo of the aftermath.

Growing up and older, we got together as much as we could. In recent years however, our connection with Alicia has been rekindled with sibling bonds growing stronger. Seeing the three of us dancing together at Brendan and Caitlyn's wedding was a most memorable moment. Peter, getting into lots of trouble from Alicia, after requesting she give her dancing feet a short rest before heading back to the dancefloor, was another memory which will not soon be forgotten.

With my brother Damian, his partner Angus and my niece and nephew

Alicia's never-ending, gravitational love has seen her adopt another brother, Angus, with whom she shares the same birthday. Caitlyn was also immediately adopted as a sister by Alicia the minute they met. Then there were two more "adopted" sisters, Bec and Emma, the mums of my children Poppy and Angus, of whom Alicia is now a very happy and proud aunty.

With her inexhaustible fountain of hugs and affection, if Alicia has decided it is your time to receive hugs, boy do you know it! Even in sweaty summertime in Cairns, nothing gets in the way of Alicia's hugs. Cooking dinner while being hugged relentlessly by her was a lovely challenge for her brothers.

If unconditional love is a person, it's Alicia! We are so proud of the amazing woman you have become, a rose born between two cheeky monkeys. We love you, sister!

Aunty Mona

When I first saw you, you were only weeks old, and had the most beautiful blond hair. You were wearing a little red dress, and cream-coloured tights and looked adorable. Already at that early age, you brought so much joy into your mum and dad's life, and also all who would come to know you.

As you grew older you had a strong love for God and was happy to talk about Him as if he were your best friend, and of course He was.

We all enjoyed the many happy occasions around your dining room, sharing meals together with lots of chatter and laughter.

I hope that this book will really bless you and the beautiful young woman you have become.

Much love, Aunty Mona

Rob and Lynne (Godparents)

Alicia, we were so happy and proud to be asked to be your godparents (all those years ago!). It was a joy and a privilege to be part of that special day when you were baptised. From the time you all moved away from Canberra, we have always loved hearing the latest news about you and have watched on with great joy as your life has unfolded across the years.

We think that you are very lucky to have been adopted by Peter and Angela who we know have given, and are continuing to give, you the best life possible.

While we have been worried about your health at various times, you have risen above these challenges and gone on to make the most of every day with gusto and persistence. You have so much to be proud of, and we too are very proud of you as your godparents.

It's very hard to believe that this year you will be turning thirty-nine, Alicia. One year before the BIG 4-0! No doubt, a big party will be organised for that special day. With lots of love from Rob and Lynne.

Dad

Well my dear Alicia, this book is almost complete, and it has been quite an adventure in the making! For me, to hold your whole life till now in view has been an amazing blessing. So thank you very much for having such a great idea to write the story of your life.

Writing this book with you has brought back so many memories, mostly very happy ones, but also reminders of some very difficult times for you, and for all who love you. At times, working on your book has also been a deeply moving and emotional experience for me.

For myself, I can't imagine life without you, and I just do not have the words to fully express how much and how deeply I love you. So, above all, I am so very grateful that we were able to adopt you, and for all the years we have already shared together.

You have such a unique personality, very loving and very caring, sensitive and attentive to others and even anticipating their needs. Your sense of fun and sense of humour always brighten my days, and, somehow, just spending time with you is very good for my soul.

I love your quirky humour, especially when you and I have those crazy party nights! Sometimes what you come out with just "cracks me up" and your mum as well.

Also, your sense of adventure and "need for speed" has not only amazed me, but also has opened up many doors to "push the boundaries" together. I will never forget those incredible moments such as parasailing in a tandem harness with you, or you screaming: "Faster Dad!" when we were already skimming across the water at high speed on various jet ski rides (while Mum wasn't looking!).

Often when I look at you, I see a smaller version of Angela, your mum and primary carer for all these years. More than anyone, she has instilled in you such a loving and caring heart which you so freely open to others, especially those who are lucky enough to be regarded by you as family or friend. You have well learnt what Angela has modelled for you every day through her constant and sacrificial love and care for you, and for me.

Alicia, you are one of a kind, an incredible gift not only to your mum and me, but to everyone. It always amazes me how you draw so much love and kindness from others. But then, when you were only two years old, Oma sent us a letter which included these words: "She will evoke the kindness that will keep you human." How true.

So, Alicia, thank you for just being you and I really look forward to seeing who you are still becoming Much love from Dad.

Mum

My Alicia.

How very glad I am that you came into my life. I certainly didn't know what our life together would be like that first time I held you in my arms. You were so tiny and our first year together was particularly difficult as you struggled in so many ways. We spent so much time in doctors' surgeries as your complex health issues were initially assessed and then regularly followed up.

Nevertheless, we also had lots of good times together which have continued through the years since.

You are a warm and caring person with a keen intuition about people. Many times I have witnessed your ability to turn someone's day from sad to happy. You have the most amazing capacity to make someone feel good about themselves, through a kind word or a compliment. It is a wonderful gift.

I love your sense of humour and sense of the ridiculous. So often you deliberately come out with a funny comment or do something really silly that has us laughing along with you. This too is a precious gift.

Your incredible love of books and learning has certainly opened up new areas of interest for me. Weather, reptiles, animals, history, ancient Egypt, archaeology—these are some of the subjects in which you have led the way for me, for Dad and for others as well. You often surprise me with your knowledge of these areas and the ease with which you can find and even cross-reference specific information.

Your love of family is also very special! No one ever has to wonder if they are important to you. This includes all those you have "adopted" as your sisters or brothers.

I think you have helped me to become a better person.

You are my gorgeous girl and my wonderful daughter, and I love you more than I can say. You have enriched my life beyond measure.

My Story … My Gift

Dear reader, I am very happy that the story of my life—so far—is now complete. I really hope you have enjoyed this little book and have found out a little more about me.

I think that my life so far has made a very big difference, especially for Mum and Dad and for my family and friends. Getting to know me seems to have had a big and very positive impact on many other people, and I really hope that this will continue, also through this book.

Today, as I am approaching my thirty-ninth birthday (something which I remind Mum and Dad about nearly every day), I am very happy being who I am and am looking forward to seeing what the future holds. I am hopeful about my future. At the same time, I am very grateful for the many years of happiness, joy and love shared with Mum and Dad, and with my family and friends; so many happy memories, only some of which could be recorded in this book.

I have already had many wonderful adventures which have also pushed my limits, and perhaps any boundaries that others might have placed on me. And there have been countless more days in which I have just been at home with Mum and Dad, enjoying the things that I like to do, with Mum always looking after me, and Dad mostly being my entertainer!

Thank you very much for reading my story. Please accept it as my little gift of love … and of hope. Cheers!

www.ingramcontent.com/pod-product-compliance
Lightning Source LLC
Chambersburg PA
CBHW041501010526
44107CB00049B/1614